mo

4192!

**DO NOT REMOVE
CARDS FROM POCKET**

89-1

4192!

A CELEBRATION OF
PETE ROSE
BASEBALL'S
RECORD-BREAKING
HITTER

BY UNITED PRESS INTERNATIONAL

CONTEMPORARY
BOOKS, INC.
CHICAGO

CONTENTS

FOREWORD

I wish I could come up with some fancy words to describe Pete Rose. But Pete Rose shouldn't be associated with fancy words anyway.

That's because he's a working man's hitter. He's a working man's man, and that's the way he loves it. Pete's the kind of guy who brings his hard hat and his lunch pail to the batter's box. He gets down and dirty—then he gets to hitting like only he knows how.

The first thing that ever impressed me about Pete's hitting when I managed him with the Reds organization is the same thing that impresses me now—he has so much concentration. He bears down on every swing. He never gives away an at-bat.

Think about that for a minute. It doesn't matter what the score is, Pete bears down like every time at bat will be his last one ever. He never gives anything away.

When you look at Pete's physical tools, you wonder how in the heck he's done everything he has. The Good Lord didn't give him an abundance of talent. I always used to say that here's a guy who can't hit, he can't throw, he can't run, and yet he's one of the greatest players in the history of the game. He always gets the job done.

That's the beauty of Pete Rose. He is living proof that if you want something bad enough and you're willing to bleed for it, then you can do it.

There'll never be another Pete Rose. You can file that. Once he's gone this game will lose something it can never replace. I'm one of the luckiest people in baseball just to have been associated with him.

Sparky Anderson
Former Manager, Cincinnati Reds
Manager, Detroit Tigers

ACKNOWLEDGMENTS

This book was a team effort by the sportswriters and photographers of United Press International, the world's premier baseball reporting service.

The pictures in this book were selected and edited by New York Photo Editor Larry DeSantis, who reviewed 60 years of brilliant work by UPI sports photographers. Some of the photos come from the Bettmann Archive which stores and catalogues UPI photos in New York. Some of the Ty Cobb photos were supplied by the Detroit Historical Society.

Most of the writing was done by UPI National Baseball Writer Mike Tully and Assistant Sports Editor Fred McMane. They were assisted by sportswriters Fred Down, Fred Lief, and Ric Van Sant. Milton Richman, UPI's senior sports columnist, also gave important advice on the production of the book. The book also draws heavily on the reporting and statistics gathering of the 50 UPI writers who work the sports beat every day.

David Tucker
UPI Sports Editor

TO CATCH A PHANTOM

Two legends face off.

The year that Ty Cobb died, Pete Rose came of age as a professional baseball hitter.

Cobb, whose .367 lifetime batting average is his claim to being recognized as the greatest hitter who ever lived, died on July 17, 1961, and that year Rose, a 20-year-old infielder for Tampa of the Class A Florida State Rookie League, led the league in hits with 160.

No one realized that 24 years later the two men would be linked together in baseball history.

Tyrus Raymond Cobb and Peter Edward Rose had very little in common as human beings and yet they shared a common bond.

On September 30, 1928, Cobb officially retired and all baseball breathed easier.

For 24 tumultuous years, Cobb had dominated baseball with a talent and a fury unmatched in its history. He entered the game in 1905 in its Neanderthal period and left in its Golden Age.

His name alone brought a torrent of passion from those who played with him. He played with a demonic rage that made his fans and fellow players regard him with fear and awe. He ran wild with spikes high on the basepaths and set stolen base records that stood for a half century. He was a big man for his era—bigger and stronger than most of his peers. He caused a baseball strike by punching a crippled fan. He had no friends and he wanted none. He slept with a gun under his pillow during the latter years of his life. When he died only one representative of baseball attended his funeral.

His enemies—and they were many—were glad to see him retire after 22 seasons. Most acknowledged him as the greatest player of his era but he also was the most hated. He left a page of major league and American League records on the books—most of which his peers and immediate successors said would never be broken.

One of the most respected of those records is his intimidating career total of 4,191 hits. In a game where only 9 men in history have ever hit over 3000—Cobb hit 4191. Now this incredible record is being challenged and is within easy reach of a man straight out of Middle America.

He is Peter Rose of Cincinnati, Ohio, and he has brought to baseball a quality that is unique. Many call it boyish enthusiasm, but "joy" is the word that better defines it; joy in one's work, in challenge and

accomplishment. It's an old word, a revered word and it's not used much anymore. But someone like Pete Rose rarely comes along in the sport of baseball.

Rose has seldom struck anyone as an awesome bundle of God-given talent. His swing is equally awkward from both sides of the plate. He has never been a homerun hitter, hitting only 158 in his career. And although he's a hustler, he has only 187 stolen bases in his career. Yet Rose runs out from under his cap more than any other player in memory. He has been the Eternal Rookie from the day he reported to the Reds in 1963 at the age of 21 until 1985 as the team's player-manager preparing to light up baseball with the number, 4,192.

NUMBERS NOT TO BE BELIEVED

Throughout his 25-year career few considered Pete Rose the greatest player in baseball history or even of his era. He has not displayed the grandeur of Babe Ruth or the grace of Joe DiMaggio. He

Left: Although Rose may not have the natural talent of a Ruth or a DiMaggio, he has carved out his place in baseball history with his mind . . . *above*: . . . and his bat.

can't hit like Ted Williams, field like Willie Mays, or run like Lou Brock.

Yet Rose has had the singular ability to beat the opposition in any given game by calling on whatever skill is needed.

Rose has plenty of talent. It is modest, however, when compared with the talents of many of the 193 men who have been accorded baseball's supreme honor: election to the Hall of Fame in Cooperstown, New York. When he joined the Reds as a wide-eyed awkward rookie in 1963, two veterans destined for the Hall of Fame looked this anachronism over and nicknamed him "Charlie Hustle."

The name became his badge of honor. Perhaps the greatest tribute that could be paid to him is that no other player in the sport has come as close to giving 100 percent in every game.

As rookie or star, Rose played any position at which he was needed. Across 23 years, he has been named to All-Star teams at first base, second base, third base, and in the outfield. In an era of grueling coast-to-coast travel across three time zones, he has played at least 136 games annually for 18 consecutive years. Hall of Famer Mickey Mantle, one of the New York Yankees' superstars, once looked at Rose's games played record and marveled, "imagine how many times he did that with a hangover," without knowing Rose rarely drank.

As one season blended into another, Rose's numbers began to add up and become records: Most games, lifetime; most singles, lifetime; most consecutive seasons playing in 100 or more games; most seasons with 200 or more hits; most seasons playing in 150 or more games; most at-bats, lifetime; most plate appearances, lifetime; most consecutive seasons with 600 or more times at bat.

The honors came, too: Rookie of the Year in 1963; National League's Player of the Year in 1968; National League's Most Valuable Player in 1973; Major League Player of the Decade in 1979. He was the American work ethic in a baseball uniform.

Young Pete and his teammates read about Cobb's death and funeral in the Florida newspapers during spring training. Rose, who is statistics oriented, read the incredible numbers: .367 lifetime batting average . . . 12 American League batting championships including nine in a row . . . 96 stolen bases in one season and 892 lifetime . . . a .420 batting average in 1911, .410 in 1912 and .401 in 1922 at the age of 35 . . . 4,191 hits . . . a .323

batting average at the age of 41 in 1928. Cobb's life recounted in the language of statistics seemed like a series of typographical errors.

There was more in the obituaries—commentaries from Cobb's contemporaries.

"I don't blame any young ballplayer who looks at the records Cobb set and refuses to believe them," said Ray Schalk, a catcher for the Chicago White Sox during Cobb's era. "If I hadn't played against that devil, I wouldn't believe them myself."

Another commentary was from Casey Stengel, who also played in Cobb's era and later managed the Yankees to a record five consecutive World Series triumphs from 1949 through 1953.

"He had the look of a wild man, a demon," said Stengel. "You knew you could never beat him because he had a mission, a mad driven mission of revenge for something or other. He must have been possessed."

Rose shook his head. How could anyone make a crusade of hatred out of playing baseball? Sure, baseball was a physical sport, not to be mistaken for tiddleywinks. The rules state that the baseline belongs to the runner and Rose played by the rules. The brushback pitch was part of a pitcher's bill of rights. It was a warning not an assault. Baseball is the summer game, played in the afternoon sun or the cool of early evening. It was a complicated game, eight defenders coordinating their abilities to assist a pitcher. But to Rose it was simple. You went out every day and played as hard as humanly possible.

Look, Rose told himself as he looked at Cobb's numbers, Ty Cobb is Ty Cobb and Pete Rose is Pete Rose and nobody will ever get us confused.

OPENING DAY, 1985

April 8, 1985, and Pete Rose, soon to be 44, player-manager of the Cincinnati Reds, peered out from the dugout at the softly falling snow in Riverfront Stadium. On the first day of the season sweet nervousness takes hold of even 10-year veterans. Knees knock just a bit and hands tremble until the National Anthem is played and the umpire says, "Play Ball."

This was Pete Rose's 23rd Opening Day but it was different from the rest. This was the beginning of his final assault on one of the most respected records of perhaps the greatest and surely the saddest baseball player in the history of the game.

Hitman Rose.

Hitman Cobb.

COBB'S MAJOR RECORDS

Tyrus Raymond Cobb was born on December 18, 1886, at Narrows, Banks County, Georgia. He died in Atlanta, Georgia, on July 17, 1961. He stood 6 feet, 1 inch and weighed 175 pounds. He threw right-handed and batted left-handed. He married Mrs. Frances Cass on September 24, 1949.

At his retirement after the 1928 season, Cobb held numerous records. They are as follows:

Major League

- Career batting average (.367)
- Most career hits (4,191)
- Most runs (2,245)
- Tied for most seasons playing with one club (22)
- Games played in one league (3,033)
- Most seasons batting over .300 (23)
- Most consecutive seasons batting over .300 (23)

American League

- Tied for most seasons played 100 or more games (19)
- Most seasons leading league in batting (12)
- Most consecutive seasons leading league in batting (9)
- Most seasons leading league in hits (8)
- Most triples (297)
- Most seasons of 200 hits or more (9)
- Most stolen bases in a season (96)
- Most career stolen bases (892)
- American league's Most Valuable Player, 1911
- First player inducted into the Hall of Fame, 1936

His lifetime statistics are as follows: 3,033 games played; 11,429 at-bats, 2,244 runs scored; 4,191 hits; 724 doubles, 297 triples; 118 home runs; 1,954 RBI; .367 average; 274 errors; .961 fielding average.

ROSE'S MAJOR RECORDS*

Pete Edward Rose and his wife Carol (Woliung) live in Cincinnati. He has three children: daughter Fawn (12–29–64); son Pete Jr. (11–16–69); and son Tyler (10–1–84).

Major League

- All-time Major League record for most games played (3,371)
- All-time Major League record for most at-bats (13,411)
- All-time Major League record for most singles (3,082)
- All-time Major League record for most hits by a switch-hitter (4,097)
- All-time Major League record for most total bases by a switch-hitter (5,559)
- All-time Major League record for most seasons of 200 or more hits (10)
- All-time Major League record for most consecutive seasons of 100 or more hits (22)
- All-time Major League record for most seasons of 600 or more at-bats (17)
- All-time Major League record for most seasons of 150 or more games (17)
- Only player in Major League history to play more than 500 games at five different positions—1B (768); 2B (628); 3B (634); LF (671); RF (595)
- Major League record for highest fielding percentage by an outfielder, lifetime, 1,000 or more games (.991)
- Major League record for playing in most winning games (1,870)

National League

- All-time NL record for most career hits (4,097)
- All-time NL record for most career doubles (726)
- Modern NL record for longest consecutive game hitting streak (44 games; June 14–July 31, 1978)

*Pre-1985 season

Rose had long since made his biggest decision of the day. Mario Soto, a right-hander from the Dominican Republic, would be his starting pitcher. If the game was postponed, Soto would simply pitch the next time.

But Rose had two missions this year. There was the Reds' drive for a title and there was Cobb. And on this Opening Day of 1985, the 52,971 fans weren't wondering whether Rose would put the hit-and-run on or when he would pull Soto.

They were there so that they would be able to say someday, "I saw Pete Rose the day he chased down Ty Cobb."

This was the challenge that Rose brought with him to the 1985 season. All at once, he would be asked to extract potential from his team, withstand the crush of publicity, and hurl his body against pitchers half his age.

During the winter, Rose had brushed aside the Ty Cobb issue, saying he would be in the lineup to hit only if he deserved to be.

Now the off-season news conferences were over and Peter Edward Rose had a ballgame to win. He made up the lineup card. Eric Davis in center. Rose at first. Dave Parker in right. Cesar Cedeno in left. Nick Esasky at third. Dave Concepcion at short. Ron Oester at second. Dann Bilardello catching. Soto pitching.

On the mound for the Expos was Steve Rogers, a veteran right-hander who had fought back from arm problems to win the Opening Day assignment. Rogers broke into the majors in 1973. By then Rose had played in five All-Star games.

Rose made his first 1985 plate appearance in the first inning, with one out, and he drew a walk. In the third inning, with two out and a runner on first base, Rose tapped back to Rogers, who threw him out.

When the fifth inning came, the game was still scoreless, and Rose came to the plate. Soto was on third, Davis on second. Rose doubled to left, scoring both runners and notching the first of the

Earlier this year: Rose predicts the day he will break Cobb's record.

final 95 hits he needed to pass Cobb. He later scored the third run of the inning.

In the seventh, Rose batted against Tim Burke, a 26-year-old right-hander. Burke was four years old when Rose got his first major-league hit. With Davis on third and one out, Rose singled to right, scoring Davis. He then removed himself for pinch-runner Eddie Milner. Two down, 93 hits to go.

The days warmed and the hits came at a familiar pace: a single against Montreal's Bill Gullickson, a pair of hits in New York, one off of Bruce Berenyi and another off of Doug Sisk. Rose's pursuit of Ty Cobb gave baseball a new race to watch. Rose was even in the baseball standings as papers dutifully carried a daily countdown of his hit totals. The National Weather Service announced it would name two hurricanes after Rose and artist Andy Warhol was commissioned to do a Rose painting. Everywhere Rose went, he gave someone the chance to say "I saw Peter Rose the year he chased down Ty Cobb." Every time he went onto the field, Pete Rose took Ty Cobb with him.

PEACH?

Cobb was born on December 18, 1886, in Narrows, Georgia. In baseball, he became known as The Georgia Peach, a nickname which had little to do with his disposition. There was nothing peachy about Cobb and his searing desire to excel. His contemporaries, both teammates and rivals, saw Cobb as a fierce whirlwind, sowing much and accepting what he reaped.

Cobb simply hated to lose and schemed to do anything possible to avoid it. He relentlessly studied his opponents, searching for weaknesses that he could exploit in the heat of a game. He ran and slid hard and expected others to do the same. With a style that made aggression seem an understatement, he tried to intimidate opponents into making mistakes when they confronted him. Quite often, they didn't disappoint him.

One down, 94 to go.

Above: The Georgia Peach at bat. *Below*: Well-known for his aggressive baserunning, Cobb, spikes flying, slides into third.

This passion to win led to incidents that linked Cobb with some of the greatest names in baseball history. In 1909, he was accused of deliberately spiking Philadelphia third baseman Home Run Baker, an accusation he always resented. When Baker was elected to the Hall of Fame in 1955, Cobb praised the choice.

During the 1909 World Series, Cobb is said to have taunted Pittsburgh Pirates Hall of Famer Honus Wagner at short by standing on first base and yelling, "Look out Krauthead. I'm coming down." Wagner wound up tagging Cobb rudely in the mouth. Cobb later called Wagner the greatest player he ever saw.

Cobb was always willing to stand up for himself, whether it was with a heckling fan, a teammate who monopolized batting practice, or an opponent that stood in his way. The fierceness of his temperament left him with few friends. He was, in the end, a lonely man.

But what a ballplayer!

Cobb broke into the big leagues in 1905 and hit .240. For the rest of his career, The Georgia Peach never hit lower than .320 As one measure of that figure, consider that five players have won American League batting titles by hitting less.

Of the nine .400 season averages achieved by American Leaguers, Cobb accounted for three. In 1911, he assembled one of the greatest seasons in baseball history. He led the league with 248 hits, 47 doubles, 24 triples, 147 runs, 144 RBI, 83 stolen bases, .621 slugging percentage, and .420 batting average.

Two more achievements illustrate Cobb's consistent hit production. First, the only year between 1907 and 1919 that Cobb failed to lead the league in hitting was 1916. That year he hit .371, but Tris Speaker batted .386.

Second, though sometimes considered a singles hitter, Cobb posted a lifetime—*lifetime*—slugging percentage of .513. In contrast Reggie Jackson won the American League slugging crown in 1976 with a .502.

Cobb finished his career with the Philadelphia

TY COBB'S STATISTICS

Year	Team	AB	H	2B	3B	HR	R	RBI	SB	AVG.
1905	Detroit	150	36	6	0	1	19	15	2	.140
1906	Detroit	350	112	13	7	1	44	41	23	.320
1907	Detroit	605	212	29	15	5	97	116	49	.350
1908	Detroit	581	188	36	20	4	88	108	39	.324
1909	Detroit	573	216	33	10	9	116	107	76	.377
1910	Detroit	509	196	36	13	8	106	91	64	.385
1911	Detroit	591	248	47	24	8	147	144	83	.420
1912	Detroit	553	227	30	23	7	119	90	61	.410
1913	Detroit	428	167	18	16	4	70	67	52	.390
1914	Detroit	345	127	22	11	2	69	57	35	.368
1915	Detroit	563	208	31	13	3	144	99	96	.369
1916	Detroit	542	201	31	10	5	113	68	68	.371
1917	Detroit	588	225	44	23	7	107	102	55	.383
1918	Detroit	421	161	19	14	3	83	64	34	.382
1919	Detroit	497	191	36	13	1	92	70	28	.384
1920	Detroit	428	143	28	8	2	86	63	14	.334
1921	Detroit	507	197	37	16	12	124	101	22	.389
1922	Detroit	526	211	42	16	4	99	99	9	.401
1923	Detroit	556	189	40	7	6	103	88	9	.340
1924	Detroit	625	211	38	10	4	115	74	23	.338
1925	Detroit	415	157	31	12	12	97	102	13	.378
1926	Detroit	233	79	18	5	4	48	62	9	.339
1927	Philadelphia (AL)	490	175	32	7	5	104	93	22	.357
1928	Philadelphia (AL)	353	114	27	4	1	54	40	5	.323
Totals		**11429**	**4191**	**724**	**297**	**118**	**2245**	**1961**	**892**	**.367**

Athletics after 22 years with Detroit. He achieved the last of his 4,191 hits on September 3, 1928. It was a double off Washington right-hander Bump Hadley. Cobb was pinch-hitting for shortstop Joe Boley in a 6–1 loss to the Senators.

Philadelphia finished in second place that year, with a 98–55 record, behind the pennant-winning New York Yankees. In 1928 Al Smith was running against Herbert Hoover for president. It was a few months short of his 42nd birthday and Ty Cobb batted .323.

Ferocity and achievement embodied the legend of Ty Cobb. He gave well to baseball. Those in the game, despite his private fury, revered him. Years after his retirement, Cobb retained an interest in the sport he had dominated so long. In 1960 he attended the New York Yankees' Old Timers' Day program and gave batting tips to Roger Maris and Mickey Mantle.

"Cobb represented the typical spirit of baseball we knew as youngsters," former basball commissioner Ford Frick said. "Baseball would not have reached its great proportions if it were not for the struggling spirit of a man like Cobb."

What would Cobb have said as Rose approached his record? Chances are it would not have been charitable.

In 1949, Cobb came back for a look at his game, attending an Old Timers' Day at Yankee Stadium. He was then 62.

As the New York press phalanx closed in on their quarry, one of their number reeled in astonishment at a gaze as clear and fierce as a tiger's. That young reporter was Fred Down, a UPI sportswriter, who later gave the following account of the confrontation.

EVERY MAN FOR HIMSELF

"He looks like he doesn't like the human race," said the one reporter to another.

"Tell us how things were in your day," a reporter asked.

"There's nothing to tell," said Cobb. "It's all

Cobb hurls himself across home plate while catcher Kritchell tries to block him—May 4, 1912.

there in the record book."

"Who helped you the most when you were a young player?" another asked.

"Nobody," Cobb said. "The veterans didn't help the young players in those days. You had to fight to get into the batting cage. It was every man for himself."

"Is it true that you sat on the dugout steps sharpening your spikes?" asked another. "I did that a couple of times for effect," Cobb replied. "The sportswriters made too much of it."

"What do you think you would hit if you were playing today?" came another question.

"About .320," he said.

"Why that low?" the startled reporter asked.

"You have to remember I'm 62 years old," said Cobb without the trace of a smile.

"What about your records?" a reporter went on. "They say records are made to be broken."

"I don't agree with that," Cobb said. "I didn't make my records to be broken."

"But, about the 4,190 hits," a reporter persisted.

"4,191," corrected Cobb.

"I'm sorry, 4,191," said the reporter. "I mean, sir, if the young fellows were to come along and take all your records except one, which would you keep?"

"They can have all the records they want except one," said Cobb. "I'll always have the .367 (lifetime batting average)."

Above: Cobb was an awe-inspiring figure who embodied the spirit of old-time baseball. *Right*: The fierce eyes of Ty Cobb—1923.

2
ROOKIE

In 1962, the Cincinnati Reds finished third in the National League. With Fred Hutchinson as their manager, they won 98 games and lost 64, narrowly missing a tie with the pennant-winning San Francisco Giants and the Los Angeles Dodgers. The Reds were a good team. They had won the pennant a year earlier, only to lose the World Series to the New York Yankees in five games.

Cincinnati's second baseman in 1962 was Don Blasingame, then 30 and in the midpoint of a 12-year major league career. He finished the season hitting .281 with 2 homers and 35 RBI. Blasingame had been acquired from San Francisco early in 1961 and had become a regular in the Reds' lineup. But 1962 was to be his only full season with the team. He would soon be gone, and Pete Rose would take his place at second. That quiet, undramatic move would launch a fabulous career and set loose the spirit that would drive a baseball dynasty.

The year that Ty Cobb was giving batting tips to Roger Maris and Mickey Mantle, a 19-year-old native of Cincinnati reported to the Geneva ballclub in the New York-Penn League. A fine athlete who showed special promise as a football player,

Rose graduated from Cincinnati's Western Hills High School in 1960. Shortly thereafter he signed with the Reds organization.

Actually, Rose's bloodlines were more impressive than his skinny frame. The son of Laverne and Harry Rose, Rose came from good athletic stock. His father, who everybody called "Pete," was a standout semi-pro football player and his uncle, Buddy Bloebaum, was a professional baseball scout, who arranged a tryout for young Pete with the Reds.

Like the father of New York Yankee Hall of Famer Mickey Mantle, Rose's dad urged his son to learn the art of switch-hitting.

Years later, as Rose closed in on the "unbreakable" record, he paid tribute to Pete Rose Sr., a banker who was always on time and imparted to his son two important American virtues—hard work and joy in work well done.

"I get all my determination, all my habits, from my father. Really. There's no question in my mind that all the good habits I've been able to develop in baseball are the same habits I had when I was a kid," said Rose.

Rose became known for his tremendous desire. Here, he outruns his cap.

"He worked at Fifth-Third Bank in Cincinnati for about 38 years. He approached his job the same way I approach being a baseball player. What I mean by that is, he was always on time, very punctual, very dedicated. Before he went home the job was done. Never would take a day off. He'd go in even if he didn't feel well. When he got his vacation he would take it and go watch me play on a daily basis. He was very dedicated, not only in sports, but to give his employer a good effort.

"It's not always 'just do the big things' and don't do the little things, because most of the time, if you do the little things they'll make you win. To be honest, I don't play baseball any differently than my father approached being a banker.

"I was lucky that he was an athlete. All the things that I do, I saw him do. He didn't tell me to do them, I saw him do them. I used to go everywhere when he played and watched him and knew how good an athlete he was because I saw him on a daily basis.

"I just picked little things up from watching him.

He didn't have to tell me. He would correct me as far as the right way to play the game, but there again, you see someone day in and day out, whether they're playing basketball, football or baseball, you just get to know them pretty well.

"It was exposure. That's the main reason I've been able to develop all the things that I think are the right way to play the game, the right way to practice, the dedication factor, the 'be on time' factor, a lot of little things that lead up to big things."

"CHARLIE HUSTLE"

The skinny kid hit .277 for Geneva in his first year as a pro in the minor league. As he matured physically and began adjusting to the professional life things went better. He hit .331 for Tampa of the Florida State League, and led the league with 160 hits and 30 triples. He also stole 30 bases and was named the minor-league player of the year.

"I was making $400 a month that year, and I

Above: A young Pete Rose with his number one fan—Dad. *Right*: Rose's trademark—a head-first slide.

owned two pairs of pants and three pairs of socks," Rose recalls. "But those were good days. We won the league championship and the owner wanted to do something for us. He bought us all lighters. And I didn't smoke."

Rose's career was beginning to warm up, though. Promoted to Macon of the South Atlantic League, he hit .330 in 1962, leading the league with 136 runs and 17 triples.

Dave Bristol, a former major-league manager, was Rose's skipper in Macon. "Around the leagues, they used to call Pete "Hollywood" because of the way he hustled," said Bristol. "Pete would just grin and run all the harder."

Word got around. Rose's drive had engaged the attention of Cincinnati manager Fred Hutchinson. During the off-season that year, he said, "If I had any guts, I'd stick Rose on second and forget about him."

Rose helped Hutchinson make up his mind with a little display of dedication during the 1963 exhibition season. Rose, with the other players not in that day's starting lineup, took batting practice on the second diamond at Al Lopez Field in Tampa, Florida. Before quitting for the day, however, he followed the advice of an organization man named Mike Ryba. "Why don't you stick around," suggested Ryba. "You might see some action."

Rose entered the game that day as a pinch runner and then delivered two straight doubles as the game stretched into extra innings.

It was about this time in his career that Rose received his baseball christening from two of the game's most revered players. In a spring training contest against the New York Yankees, Rose drew a base on balls and did his usual all-out scamper to first base. Yankee stars Whitey Ford and Mickey Mantle noticed and began riding the youngster.

"Hey, you, Charlie Hustle," they said. The nickname stayed with him.

On April 8, 1963, President Kennedy watched in D.C. Stadium as the Baltimore Orioles beat the Washington Senators 3–1. And in Cincinnati's Crosley Field, Peter Edward Rose was about to

embark on his first Major League season. The Opening Day lineup, which looked like this:

Leo Cardenas, ss
Pete Rose, 2b
Vada Pinson, rf
Frank Robinson, lf
Gordy Coleman, 1b
Johnny Edwards, c
Gene Freese, 3b
Tommy Harper, cf
Jim O'Toole, p

Although Cincinnati beat Pittsburgh 5–2. Rose went 0-for-3 and committed an error. He walked in the first inning and scored on Robinson's home run.

Five days later, Rose got his first big league hit, a triple off Pittsburgh right-hander Bob Friend. The Reds lost that game 12–4. Only 4191 hits to go.

THE ROOKIE DOESN'T STAND A CHANCE

Some common rookie problems developed that year. Rose wasn't hitting. He was 3-for-23.

"He was fine in spring training, " said Hutchinson. "But once the season began he was too overanxious. It was tough playing at home and he was on the spot."

After a two-week rest designed to make him relax and get acquainted with the League, the Reds were now committed to this raw "Charlie" as their second baseman.

"The reason Hutch liked me," Rose said 23 seasons later, "was because of the way I played. So, I had already learned the way to approach the game before I met Hutch. But, I do owe a lot to Hutch because he gave me the opportunity to play. He went out on a limb to give me the second base job. But evidently he thought I deserved it.

"In '62, Blasingame had a .281 batting average, which was the highest of his career, but in '63 Hutch chose me. He went out on a limb, I mean Hutch did. But he got to see me win Rookie of the Year. Unfortunately, a lot of the other things I've accomplished, Hutch didn't get to see. But knowing Hutch like I did, I feel he's watching somewhere. I guess he feels good about giving me a chance to play.

"It was a team of cliques," Rose said of the '63 Reds. "Me, I was the brash kid. They rejected me. But I was on Cloud Nine and didn't even realize it. A writer took a poll: Yes or no, did the players think Pete Rose was going to make it? Out of 17 players, only one said I would make it. Don Blasingame." Rose attracted other important believers, though.

Frank Robinson, who had won the National League MVP Award in 1961 and who would later capture the prize in the other league, noticed him. So did Vada Pinson, an established star who would wind up his career with 2757 career hits.

By May of 1963, the circle of admirers was growing. Sportswriters were drawn to Rose's flamboyant aggressiveness and his climbing batting average. None as yet had a strong inkling about what this youngster would become but for the moment he made great copy. He played old fashioned baseball, he ran non-stop and he left images that stuck in the mind's eye. One of them—that of the boy running out from under his cap—may be with us as long as there is baseball lore.

In May, UPI portrayed him as a throwback to the St. Louis Cardinals "Gashouse Gang" of the late 1930s because of his intense style:

"When Rose gets hit by a pitch, he goes to first base faster than most players legging out an infield hit. When he triples, he runs out from under his cap. Someday he is likely to reach second on a base on balls.

"But Cincinnati manager Fred Hutchinson doesn't care how often Rose's cap falls off or how fast he gets to first base just so he continues to get there as often as he has in recent weeks . . ."

Writers also relished this 22-year-old's ability to deliver the solid one-liner. When asked about his hustling, Rose replied: "I don't run to first on walks just to show off, but come to think of it, there's no sense hanging around home plate when I could be on first base."

Baseball was different when Rose entered it in 1963. The National League had 10 teams, having just expanded to Houston and New York the previous season. The Los Angeles Dodgers won the pennant, with Sandy Koufax leading the pitching staff. The Hall of Fame left-hander enjoyed perhaps his greatest year, going 25–5 with a 1.88 ERA and 306 strikeouts. He won both the MVP and the Cy Young Awards.

Koufax pitched one of three no-hitters in baseball that season. He blanked San Francisco 8–0 on

May 11, Don Nottebart of Houston thwarted Philadelphia 4–1 on May 17 and San Francisco's Hall of Famer Juan Marichal shut down Houston 1–0 on June 15.

Tommy Davis led the Dodgers and the league with a .326 batting average. Frank Howard supplied the power with 28 home runs. Hank Aaron and Willie McCovey tied for the league lead in homers with 44 apiece.

In the American League, Hall of Fame left-hander Whitey Ford went 24–7 to pace the Yankees to their fourth straight pennant. Catcher Elston Howard hit .287 with 28 homers and 85 RBI to win the MVP.

The National League won the All-Star game, played in Cleveland, 5–3. In the World Series, Los

Charlie Hustle sprints to first base.

Angeles swept the Yankees in four games. Koufax won two games. The Yankees scored only four runs in the entire series. Yankee first baseman Joe Pepitone lost a throw in the white of the shirtsleeve crowd, leading to the winning run in the final game.

ROOKIE OF THE YEAR

The Reds managed to go 86–76, good for fifth place. Pinson hit .313 with 22 homers and 106 RBI. Robinson had 21 homers and 91 RBI. A 23-year-old right-hander named Jim Maloney blossomed with a 23–7 record.

During the off-season, Rose landed in the news again. Baseball seemed unimportant at the time. The nation was trying to reassemble itself in the grim days after the assassination of President Kennedy. One day after the burial, UPI sent the following dispatch:

FORT KNOX, Ky., Nov. 26 (UPI)—Pvt. Pete Rose was on K.P. duty waxing a kitchen floor when he got the news today that he had been named National League Rookie of the Year.

Rose, in his third week of Army basic training in a six-month program, received all but three votes in the balloting of the Baseball Writers Association of America in the 10 National League cities.

Hy Hurwitz, secretary of the Baseball Writers' announced in Boston that Rose got 17 votes, New York Met infielder Ron Hunt two, and Philadelphia pitcher Ray Culp one. Rose is only the second Cincinnati player to be so honored. Frank Robin-

son won the award in 1956.

Rose, a "sleeper" who wasn't placed on the Reds' roster until the night before the season opened, played in 157 games and batted .273. Among his 170 hits last season were six homers, nine triples, and 25 doubles.

As leadoff man and one of the fastest runners on the club, Rose stole 13 bases and scored 101 times. He drove in 41 runs.

At Fort Knox, Rose is a platoon guide in Company E, 11th Battalion, third training brigade. As such, he is the ranking Army rookie in his company of 68 soldiers, but that doesn't exempt him from K.P. duty. He doesn't know yet what the Army will do with him upon completion of basic training, but expects to find out next week . . .

Above: Private Pete Rose accepts congratulations from his platoon sergeant on being named 1963 National League Rookie of the Year. *Right*: Shall we dance?

(The story went on to say that Rose wasn't too surprised, but "I didn't think I'd win by such a big margin.")

During the winter, Rose married Karolyn Engelhardt, his hometown sweetheart. He also attended a testimonial dinner for Stan Musial, and the Cardinal great failed to recognize him.

"It's me, Stan, me, Pete Rose," the young second baseman said.

"Pete, what are you doing in that army uniform?" a puzzled Musial asked.

The incident might have been an omen. When Rose returned to baseball in 1964, not everything went well. He hit only .269 and dropped significantly in almost every offensive category.

In mid-season, the Reds named Dick Sisler as interim manager for Hutchinson, who was ill with cancer. Sisler was no particular fan of Rose's glove and occasionally used Chico Ruiz at second. The acting manager also invited Rose for a private talk when the youngster seemed reluctant to work out at third base.

The Reds finished one game behind St. Louis. They tied for second with the Philadelphia Phillies, who blew the pennant with a late-season collapse. The Cardinals beat the Yankees in a seven-game World Series. Fred Hutchinson died on November 12 and Sisler became the full-time manager of the Reds.

Rose played winter ball to improve his fielding. After two years in the big leagues, he had known triumph and decline. He did not care for the decline. Not at all. The next season, he would come back to full power.

STAR

In 1965 Rose finally came into his own. Among the 50 players at the 1965 All-Star Game in Minnesota, only Rose was still active in 1985 when the game headed back there for its annual competition. In the '65 contest Pete Rose, starting second baseman for the National League, went 0 for 2 with a walk and a sacrifice. Two future Hall of Famers played prominent roles: Sandy Koufax was the winning pitcher and Harmon Killebrew hit a two-run fifth inning homer for the American League to tie the score 5–5. The All-Star berth and the 6–5 victory for the Nationals were the first of many accomplishments for Rose that season.

He played in all 162 games, batting .312 on 209 base hits and he collected his 500th major-league hit, a single off New York's Al Jackson on September 16. He was on his way to nine consecutive years of hitting over .300.

One statistic shaped up poorly though: the Reds finished in fourth place with an 84–73 record, well behind the Dodgers. In the three subsequent years they wound up seventh, fourth, and fourth. Rose's own career was blossoming but he was denied the satisfaction of team triumph. In later years, he would extol the pleasure of winning with a team above all other graces of the game.

The 1965 Reds were not remarkable but they were on the threshold of change. The farm system produced three Rookie of the Year players during the '60s: Rose, Tommy Helms, and Johnny Bench. From 1965 to 1970, the team traded well, acquired the right manager and found a general manager, Bob Howsam, who would make a series of brilliant deals.

Fans may disagree about who made the engine run, but two facts suggest that Rose was the fuel. He was there at the beginning and his consistent production came closest to symbolizing the relentless force that became "The Big Red Machine."

THE DYNASTY GATHERS

The 1970–76 Cincinnati Reds, nicknamed The Big Red Machine, was arguably one of the finest teams of athletes in the history of baseball. The parts came from many sources—from the farm, from trades, from surprise performances, but they were fused by the ally of all dynasties—time, good

Rose eyes the opposing team with his usual intensity.

slow time.

• In 1965, the year that Rose blossomed into a .300 hitter, the Reds had a 23-year-old Cuban prospect stationed at first base. Playing in 104 games, the young man hit .260 with 12 homers and 47 RBI. The young man's name was Tony Perez, and he would be the RBI man when the Reds entered their glory years in the '70s.

• In 1966, Rose hit .313 with 16 homers and 70 RBI. A new face arrived in the Cincinnati infield. Tommy Helms played third base, hit .284 and was named Rookie of the Year. Helms would eventually help the Reds to the 1970 pennant.

• In 1967, as Howsam took over the general manager's chair, Rose underwent the first of many position changes. He found himself in left field because the team needed room for the bat of first baseman Lee May. Helms switched to second base and Perez went to third. May, who had been with the team since 1965, hit .265 with 12 homers and 57 RBI while playing 81 games at first. The ease with which Rose changed positions was to become one of the talents that would prolong his career and keep alive the quest for Cobb's record. Rose batted .301 and appeared in the All-Star Game at second base. A 19-year-old catcher from Binger, Oklahoma, appeared in 26 games. The catcher's name was Johnny Bench. Rookie right-hander Gary Nolan went 14–8 with a 2.58 ERA.

• In 1968 came the most dramatic event in the Reds' rise. Bench was installed as the Reds' regular catcher. He hit .275 with 15 homers and 82 RBI, and won the Rookie of the Year award. Rose changed positions again, this time moving to right field. Although he missed the All-Star Game because of injury, he reached the 1000-hit mark on June 26 against New York's Dick Selma, and captured the first of his three batting titles with a .335 batting average. On June 11, the Reds pulled off a solid trade, landing shortstop Woody Woodward, and pitchers Clay Carroll and Tony Cloninger from Atlanta for Milt Pappas, Ted Davidson and Bob Johnson.

• In 1969, the improvements began to show. The major leagues went to a six-team division format and the Reds finished third in the National League West, four games behind first-place Atlanta. Pinson had been traded in the off-season for Wayne Granger and Bobby Tolan. Granger went 9–6 with a 2.79 ERA and Tolan hit .305 with 21 homers and 93 RBI as the center fielder. Jim Merritt arrived from Minnesota and went 17–9. Rose stayed in right field, played left field in the All-Star Game and won his second straight batting title, hitting

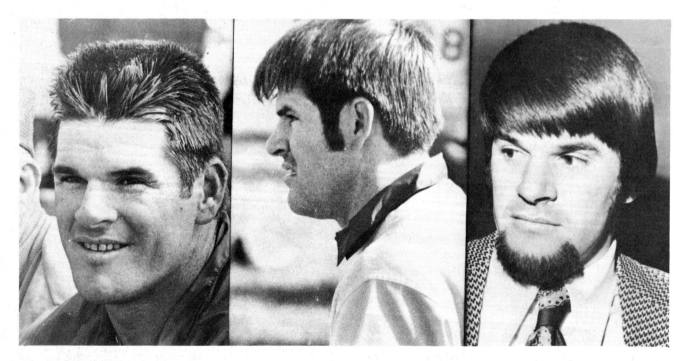

Above: The many faces of Pete Rose: although his looks changed through the years, his stats stayed consistent. (Left to right) 1970, '71, '72. *Right*: The Big Red Machine, 1970. (Left to right) Bobby Tolan, Johnny Bench, Tony Perez, Lee May, and Pete Rose.

.348. May hit 38 homers, Perez 37, Bench 26. The pennant-winning team was almost in place.

• In 1970 Rose turned 29 years old. He had been in the majors for seven years. He had 1,327 hits. Nevertheless, he had not yet played in October. The Reds were still making moves, though. They acquired Jim McGlothlin and Pedro Borbon from California. They promoted a 21-year-old right-hander named Wayne Simpson, who went 14–3, and a fire-balling left-hander named Don Gullett, who struck out 76 batters in 78 innings. They moved 22-year-old outfielder Bernie Carbo into left field and he hit .310 with 21 homers.

The Reds were two moves away from power. In 1970 they made them both. The first was the signing of a 21-year-old shortstop from Aragua, Venezuela—Dave Concepcion.

The first time Rose saw Concepcion, he wise-cracked: "Kid, there's no way you're ever gonna pull a muscle with that body you've got. You're all bones."

Concepcion, then only 155 pounds, split the shortstop duty with Woodward in 1970. It was the beginning of an outstanding career in which Concepcion helped anchor one of baseball's greatest teams.

The other infielder to join the team was a 36-year-old second baseman from Bridgewater, South Dakota, with a .218 lifetime batting average. He effected a remarkable change in the Reds. The infielder had not come to *play* second base. He came to manage the team. Sparky Anderson became a Cincinnati Red.

"I sure as heck wasn't doing much good as a player, " Anderson says now. "And I was getting worse. So I figured I could only improve by becoming a manager."

Anderson was right. He managed Toronto of the International League, Rock Hill of the Western Carolina League, St. Petersburg of the Florida State League, Modesto of the California League, and Asheville of the Southern League. He joined the San Diego Padres as a coach in 1969. And on October 9, 1969, he was named manager of the

Cincinnati Reds.

"I never even thought about managing," he says. "In 1963, I played for Toronto in the Phillies' organization and didn't have much of a year. I was packing my bags at the end of the season and the Toronto general manager came over and asked if I would like to manage the team next year. I really thought he was kidding.

"He convinced me he was serious and I decided to try. It meant I could stay in baseball without embarrassing myself. I certainly didn't mind not playing anymore."

They had Rose, Bench, Perez, and Anderson. They would soon be moving into their brand new Riverfront Stadium. Next came the tremendous focus of desire and skill that transforms a mere collection of players into a great team.

ROSE AT 1500

Cincinnati won the National League West by a persuasive 14½ games in 1970. Playing right field, Rose batted .316 with 15 homers and 52 RBI. On August 29 he reached the 1,500-hit mark with a single off Carl Morton at Montreal. It marked his sixth straight year batting over .300 and gave him more than 200 hits for the fifth time in six seasons.

Rose played in his fourth All-Star Game, this one in Cincinnati, and went 1 for 3. That one hit also involved him in one of the biggest controversies of his career. With the score tied 4–4 in the 12th inning, Rose was on base when Jim Hickman singled. Representing the winning run, Rose charged the plate in customary fashion—hellbent. He crashed into 23-year-old Cleveland catcher Ray Fosse as the ball arrived at home. The catcher suffered a shoulder injury. Fosse, then in his first full major league season, came back to finish the year hitting .307 but the injury marked the beginning of a decline. Hard luck injuries beset him throughout his 12-year career and he never regained his former grace.

Critics charged that Rose had been unnecessarily rough in what amounted to an exhibition game. Rose's reply was that he was playing the All-Star Game the way he played every other game—hard. Like no other, the play crystalized Rose's image as the fiercest competitor of his time.

In a controversial play, Rose barrels into catcher Ray Fosse in the 12th inning of the 1970 All-Star game.

The 1970 season was a good one for Rose's teammates, too. At the age of 22, Bench led the league with 45 homers and 148 RBI. Perez hit 40 homers and drove in 129 runs. May wasn't far behind with 34 homers and 94 RBI.

Nolan went 18–7 with a 3.26 ERA. Merritt was 20–12, 4.08 and McGlothlin 14–10, 3.58. Carroll had 16 saves. Granger led the league with 35. The Reds won 102 games and lost 60.

Cincinnati and Pittsburgh met in the National League playoffs, with the Reds winning the best-of-five series in three games. Rose singled home the game-winning run as Cincinnati captured the opener 3–0 in 10 innings. Nolan was the winner with Carroll earning a save.

Rose hit .231 in his first playoff, and the Reds were on their way to their first World Series in nine years.

The Reds met the Orioles who had been denied the title in 1969 by the Miracle Mets. The Orioles rolled through the series in five games. The Reds may not have been inferior to the Baltimore club but Oriole star Brooks Robinson tipped the balance between the two teams.

Robinson batted .429 and etched the Series into memory with fabulous plays at third base. Rose hit .250, going 5 for 20 with a double, a homer, and two RBI.

In 1971, the Reds slipped to fourth place 11 games behind division-winning San Francisco. Though the season was an unsuccessful one, it contained elements that would contribute to later triumphs. First, the Reds made a trade with the Giants, acquiring outfielder George Foster for shortstop Frank Duffy and pitcher Vern Geishert. The trade altered the balance of power in the division for years. Foster developed into a feared power hitter and the Giants failed to contend without him.

Rose batted .304, his seventh straight season above .300. He played in his fifth All-Star Game but did not bat. In that game, Oakland's Reggie Jackson hit a home run off the transformer in Detroit's Tiger Stadium.

After the season, the Reds made still another fabulous trade. On November 29, they acquired second baseman Joe Morgan who was to win two consecutive MVP awards, third baseman Denis Menke, pitcher Jack Billingham, and outfielders Cesar Geronimo and Ed Armbrister.

The trades, plus the return of outfielder Bobby Tolan, injured with a torn Achilles tendon, forced still another position switch for Rose. Everytime Rose switched positions, his production never faltered. His average remained above .300, and he became a team leader. Now he was being asked to switch once more. Rose shrugged off the move.

"I'm more worried about the increasing numbers of good left-handed pitchers who are coming into the league," he said. "It means that I'm going to have to take a lot more batting practice from the right side of the plate."

The batting practice clearly proved effective. In 1972, Rose led the league with 198 hits, and topped .300 for the eighth straight season. He failed to appear in the All-Star Game but the Reds won the National League Western Division by 10½ games.

'72 SERIES, ANOTHER NEAR MISS

Rose starred in the playoffs against Pittsburgh, batting .450 as the Reds captured the pennant, three games to two. But again, Cincinnati was foiled in the World Series, this time by the unorthodox A's of Oakland. The A's, a blend of handlebar moustaches, speed, defensive prowess, and stingy but effective hitting, won the first of three straight World Series titles, capturing the series in seven games. Rose batted only .214 going 6 for 28.

By now, Rose was being mentioned as a possible Hall of Famer. He was 31 years old and had 1,922 hits. By playing six or seven more seasons at past form, he could possibly reach 3,000 hits and the virtual automatic Hall of Fame berth that goes with that milestone.

In 1973, Rose went a long way toward reaching that goal. He was also beset by team disappointment and personal controversy along the way.

The Reds won their third National League West title in four years, going 99–63 to outdistance Los Angeles by 3½ games. Rose won his third batting crown, at .338. He went 0 for 3 in the All-Star Game at Kansas City. He achieved a career-high 230 hits and he reached the 2,000 mark on June 19 with a single off Ron Bryant at San Francisco.

"He sure didn't waste any time starting after the next 1,000," said Sparky Anderson after Rose doubled two innings later in the same game.

"My goal is still 3,000 hits and hitting .300 or better for 10 straight years," said Rose, who was 32 at the time. "I've got a young body. I take care of it. I don't smoke. And when I do have a drink, it's not very often or very much.

"I really don't like to think about my 3,000th hit. Besides, when I get close to it, it'll mean my playing career will be nearing an end."

The Reds post-season agonies continued. They never got a chance to capture the World Series because they never got there. The New York Mets, who survived a wacky East Division race to win with an 82–79 record, beat them in a five-game playoff.

Rose hit .381 with two homers. He also found controversy in Game 3 when his hard slide into shortstop Bud Harrelson while attempting to break up a double play led to a fight.

When the inning ended and Rose resumed his place in the outfield, fans threw debris at him. Anderson pulled the Reds off the field. A contingent of Mets, fearing a forfeit in a game they led 9–2, went out to left field to calm the fans.

In Cobbian rhetoric, Rose defended his actions.

"I'm not sorry about anything," Rose said after the game. "Me sliding hard into Harrelson trying to break up a double play was baseball the way it's supposed to be played. I'm no damn litle girl out there. I'm supposed to give the fans their money's worth and play hard and try to bust up double plays—and shortstops."

"I didn't think it was a clean play at the time,"

Above: Rose, playing left field, is up against the fence as the opposition hits a homer in the fifth game of the 1972 World Series. *Next three pages*: The drama unfolds in Game 3 of the 1973 World Series as Rose's slide into the Mets' Bud Harrelson results in a bench-clearing brawl and provokes the fans.

Harrelson says. "It was a big game; a competitive atmosphere. He was all fired up. He was always doing things to fire up his team. He didn't want to apologize. He probably felt, in his mind, he didn't have to apologize. He likes to play hard. He hit me after the play was over.

"We don't have any animosity. It just happened and it's over. I played with him in '79 in Philadelphia. We laughed about it over the winter. It was on national television. Like the Fosse thing that happened in the All-Star Game. If it's a regular game it's nothing."

Rose hit a game-winning homer the next day, but the Mets took the series.

In 1974, both Rose and the Reds faltered. Rose hit .284 and fell short of his goal to hit .300 for 10 straight seasons. He appeared in his seventh All-Star Game. The Reds never did quite catch the Dodgers, who went to the World Series and became Oakland's third straight victim.

Rose was now 33. He had played 12 big-league seasons. He had appeared in three championship series, and two World Series. He had 2,337 hits. Most players would gladly call that a career. But for Rose, the past was only prelude.

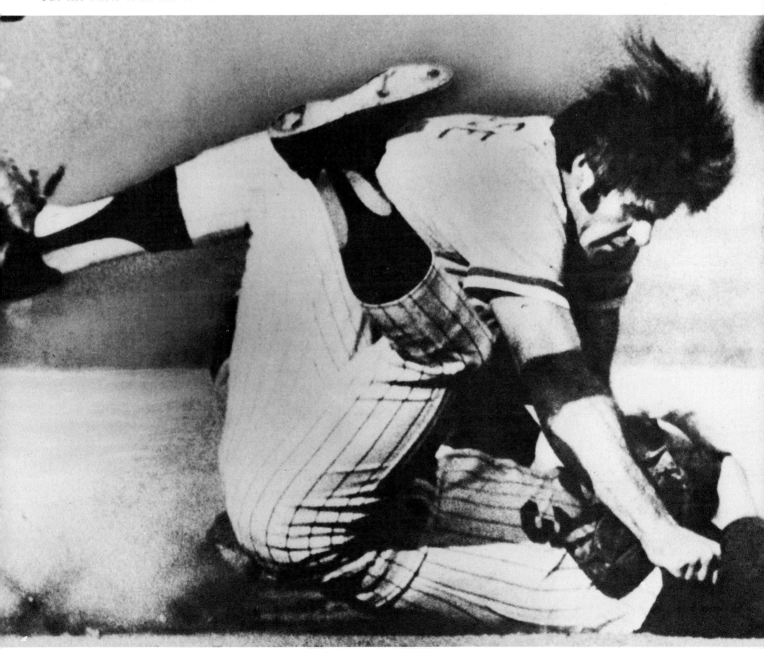

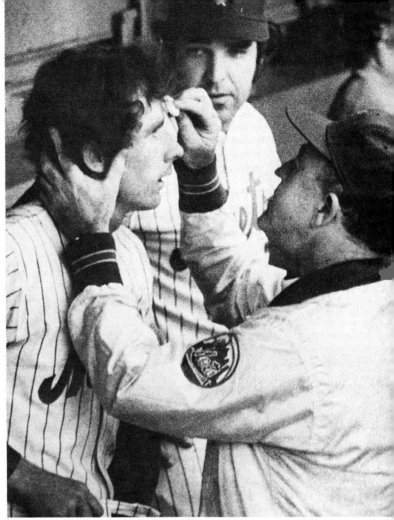

THE CHAMPIONSHIP YEARS

The 1975 season will always be firmly etched in Pete Rose's mind. It began on a sour note and ended with the sweet taste of champagne. It also provided him with *the* most memorable game and one of the most memorable hits of his career—a hit that did not count in his quest of Cobb's record.

Although he would wear a world championship ring for the first time in his career in 1975, the months leading up to the start of the season were not pleasant ones for Rose because of his first rift with Cincinnati management.

The trouble began when the Reds mailed Rose a new contract for the 1975 season, asking him to take a sizeable salary cut from his $155,000 a year contract. Rose believed the Reds were personally blaming him for the club's second place finish just because he had hit under .300 for the first time in 10 years.

"I disagree that I had a bad year," Rose said. "I did a lot of things I don't normally do that contributed to the team."

Rose pointed to his career high and league-leading 45 doubles and 106 walks. He also cited the fact he was on base more than any other player in the major leagues and set a career fielding record.

"I miss .300 for the first time in 10 years and I'm suddenly out of shape and a fatboy. Well, I didn't miss a game in 1974," Rose said. "The law of averages caught up with me. You can't hit .300 every year. I'm 32 and I feel good. I've had some good years, and I think I have some good ones left."

Once again Rose proved to be prophetic. Not only did he bounce back to hit .317 but he led the league in runs scored for the third time (112), collected more than 200 hits for the seventh time (210), and led the league in doubles (47) for the second consecutive year.

His personal statistics certainly stood out, but it was his willingness to move to yet another position that turned the Reds into the most feared power in baseball.

CINCINNATI, May 2 (UPI)—Pete Rose, Cincinnati Reds three-time batting champion, will make his season's debut at third base Saturday night in the second of the three-game series with the Atlanta Braves.

At long last a jubilant Rose celebrates a championship.

With Rose moving to third, Danny Driessen will take over the left field spot.

"I'm just hoping Pete will do an adequate job," said Reds' manager Sparky Anderson. "I don't expect him to be spectacular."

A MOVE TO THIRD AND THE CROWN AT LAST

The Reds had tried Rose at third briefly in 1966 to make room for Tommy Helms, but the experiment failed and Rose was returned to second shortly after the season began with Helms shifting to third. Helms went on to become Rookie of the Year and the next year became the Reds' regular second baseman with Rose shifting to left.

Anderson, figuring Rose was now mature enough to handle the move, asked him to give third base another try because he wanted to get more offense into the lineup. George Foster, Ken Griffey, Cesar Geronimo and Driessen were all talented hitters who were ready to make their mark.

Rose was more than adequate at third. He went 39 consecutive games without an error and in his first 65 games committed only five miscues. Moreover, he came to like the position.

"I love to play third," he said. "You know why? Cause I get to touch the ball after each out. I like to throw it around the infield. I like to touch the ball every chance I get. Third base is more fun than the outfield. I feel more part of the game. Closer to it."

Rose's ability to adjust to third base was a key to the club's success. It enabled Foster to get into 134 games and he hit .300 with 23 home runs and 78 RBI. Griffey, in his first full season, played in 132 games and hit .305. Geronimo became the regular center fielder and sparkled defensively while batting .257 in 148 games.

Seldom has a team dominated the way the Reds did in 1975. Despite a pitching staff that did not include a 20-game winner and only one starter with an earned run average under 3.00 (Don Gullett), they won the National League West by 20 games, compiling a 108–54 record. They clinched the division on September 7, the earliest clinching date in major league history.

While Rose was the gasoline that fueled the "Big Red Machine," Joe Morgan was the sparkplug. Little Joe hit .327, belted 17 home runs, drove in 94 runs, scored 107 runs, led the league in walks with 132, and fielded his position flawlessly. He was named the league's Most Valuable Player, marking the fourth time in six years that a member of the Reds had won National League MVP honors.

The Reds met the Pittsburgh Pirates, winners of the National League East, in the playoffs, but it was no contest. With Rose hitting .357, they swept

Left: Rose receives the S. Rae Hickok Professional Athlete of the Year Award, January 1976. *Above:* The controversial play in the 10th inning of Game 3 of the 1975 World Series: Boston catcher Carlton Fisk collides with Reds' Ed Armbister, and Cincinnati wins 6-5.

BASEBALL'S GREATEST TEAM?
1975 CINCINNATI REDS STATISTICS

BATTING

	AB	HR	RBI	AVG.
Perez	511	20	109	.282
Morgan	498	17	94	.327
Concepcion	507	5	49	.274
Rose	662	7	74	.317
Griffey	463	4	46	.305
Geronimo	501	6	53	.257
Foster	463	23	78	.300
Bench	530	28	110	.283
Driessen	210	7	38	.281
Rettenmund	188	2	19	.239
Chaney	160	2	26	.219
Flynn	127	1	20	.268

PITCHING

	IP	W	L	ERA
Nolan	211	15	9	3.16
Billingham	208	15	10	4.11
Norman	188	12	4	3.73
Gullett	160	15	4	2.42
Darcy	131	11	5	3.57
Borbon	125	9	5	2.95
Kirby	111	10	6	4.70
Carroll	96	7	4	2.63
McEnaney	91	5	2	2.47
Eastwick	90	5	3	2.60

the Pirates in three games and in the World Series met the Boston Red Sox, a surprise playoff winner over Baltimore in the American League.

Many baseball experts foresaw the World Series as a mismatch. The Reds, they argued, had far too much talent for the upstart Red Sox. They couldn't have been more wrong. The 1975 World Series turned out to be a classic, one that ranks with the best of all-time. And it belonged to Pete Rose.

This is the kind of World Series it was:

- Five games in the Series were decided by one run and in four of those five games the winning run scored in the ninth inning or later.
- In six of the seven games, a team that was trailing at some point in the game bounced back to win.

The Red Sox, behind the five-hit pitching of a cigar-chomping Cuban named Luis Tiant, won the first game 6-0 but the Reds rebounded to win the second game, 3-2, by scoring two runs in the ninth, with Griffey doubling home the winning run.

In the third game, which the Reds won 6-5, a record six home runs were hit, but it was a controversial 10th inning bunt by Cincinnati's Ed Armbrister that proved to be the decisive play.

Cesar Geronimo led off the 10th with a single and Armbrister bunted in front of the plate attempting to sacrifice. Boston catcher Carlton Fisk collided with Armbrister while fielding the ball and his hurried throw to second went into center field, allowing Geronimo to advance to third and Armbrister to take second.

Fisk claimed Armbrister had interfered with him, but home plate umpire Larry Barnett disallowed the interference claim, and the Reds won the game later in the inning on a single by Morgan.

Boston, behind Tiant, came back to win game four, 5–4, but the Reds got a pair of homers from Tony Perez in the fifth game and took it, 6–2.

Then came game six. Many baseball historians regard game six as the greatest World Series contest ever played.

The Reds, needing a victory to win their first World Series since 1940, led 6–3 entering the last of the eighth when Boston's Bernie Carbo came through with a record-tying second pinch-hit homer of the Series, a three-run shot to tie the score.

Each team then took turns preventing the other from scoring with spectacular defensive plays. The Red Sox threatened in the ninth but Foster threw out Denny Doyle at the plate. Boston right fielder Dwight Evans prevented the Reds from taking the lead in the 11th when he made a leaping catch to rob Morgan of a two-run homer.

Before Morgan's at-bat in the 11th, Rose stepped to the plate and turned to Fisk.

"Wow, man," Rose said. "I don't know who'll win this but isn't it great just to be here."

An inning later, with the clock striking midnight, Fisk ended the contest by rocketing a long blast off Pat Darcy that struck the foul pole above the left field fence.

If poetic justice had been served the Red Sox would have won the seventh game and been crowned world champions. And maybe if they had had Pete Rose on their side they would have won it. But the Reds had Rose and he proved to be the catalyst in the final game.

With the Red Sox nursing a 3–2 lead in the seventh inning, Rose singled home the tying run, a hit he lists among the biggest of his career. Cincinnati then won the game in the ninth when Morgan delivered a two-out, run-scoring bloop single to center.

When it came down to deciding who should take

home the sports car as the Most Valuable Player of the Series, a panel of sportswriters unanimously selected Rose, who collected 10 hits in 27 at-bats for a .370 average.

There were more post-season awards that year for Rose. He was named winner of the S. Rae Hickok Professional Athlete of the Year Award and *Sports Illustrated*'s Sportsman of the Year Award, an honor he didn't feel he deserved.

"I am not a good sportsman," he said. "If I get my rear end kicked, I don't congratulate the guy who did it. I go to the dressing room and kick the door off my locker."

ROSE ON WINNING

Rose is often portrayed in the media as a stereotypic jock—splendid on the field but devoid of intellect when off. But as Rose, in 1985, reminisces about the pleasures and triumphs of the '75 championship, one can find embedded in his words, the athlete describing a code of ethics that philosophers, poets, and psychiatrists have subscribed to.

"There's no question in my mind that my three proudest possessions are my World Series rings, and I have every award there is," Rose says. "Awards are just things that get you to a certain level pay-wise. The real rewards are what happens in the end for a team. I just think it's very important to emphasize winning; how important it is to win. It should always be 'we,' not 'I.' I've always lived with that motto and I believe in that motto.

"All my highs and lows in my big league career have been playoff and World Series competition. That's the way it should be with every player.

"I especially remember the '75 championship because that was the first one. No matter how long you play this game, you remember your first hit or your first world championship. And '75 happened to be my first world championship, and I'll always remember that."

THE AGE OF BASEBALL MILLIONAIRES

During the 1975 season pitchers Dave McNally of the Baltimore Orioles and Andy Messersmith of the Los Angeles Dodgers played without signed contracts and at the end of the season argued that they should be granted free agency on the grounds that they were no longer under contractual obligation to the club.

Game 6 of the 1975 World Series is one of the classics in all baseball. Below is the boxscore of that contest:

CINCINNATI	AB	R	H	BI	BOSTON	AB	R	H	BI
Rose, 3b	5	1	2	0	Cooper, 1b	5	0	0	0
Griffey, rf	5	2	2	2	Drago, p	0	0	0	0
Morgan, 2b	6	1	1	0	Miller	1	0	0	0
Bench, c	6	0	1	1	Wise, p	0	0	0	0
Perez, 1b	6	0	2	0	Doyle, 2b	5	0	1	0
Foster, lf	6	0	2	2	Yastrzemski, lf	6	1	3	0
Concepcion, ss	6	0	1	0	Fisk, c	4	2	2	1
Geronimo, cf	6	1	2	1	Lynn, cf	4	2	2	3
Nolan, p	0	0	0	0	Petrocelli, 3b	4	1	0	0
Cheney	1	0	0	0	Evans, 3b	5	0	1	0
Norman, p	0	0	0	0	Burleson, ss	3	0	0	0
Billingham, p	0	0	0	0	Tiant, p	2	0	0	0
Armbrister	0	1	0	0	Moret, p	0	0	0	0
Carroll, p	0	0	0	0	Carbo, lf	2	1	1	3
Crowley	1	0	1	0					
Borbon, p	1	0	0	0					
Eastwick, p	0	0	0	0					
McEnaney, p	0	0	0	0					
Driessen	1	0	0	0					
Darcy, p	0	0	0	0					
Totals	**50**	**6**	**14**	**6**	**Totals**	**41**	**7**	**10**	**7**

Flied out for Nolan in third; walked for Billingham in fifth; singled for Carroll in sixth; homered for Moret in eighth; flied out for McEnaney in tenth; flied out for Drago in 11th.

None out when winning run scored.

Cincinnati	000 030 210	000—6
Boston	300 000 030	001—7

Cincinnati

E — Burleson.	-3	1	0	0	1	1
Carroll	1	1	0	0	0	0
Borbon	2	1	2	2	2	1
Eastwick	1	2	1	1	1	2
McEnaney	1	0	0	0	1	0
Darcy (L)	2	1	1	1	0	1

Boston

Tiant	7	11	6	6	2	5
Moret	1	0	0	0	0	0
Drago	3	1	0	0	0	1
Wise (W)	1	2	0	0	0	1

Tiant pitched to 1 batter in 8th; Borbon pitched to 2 batters in 8th; Eastwick pitched to 2 batters in 9th; Darcy pitched to one batter in 12th.

HBP—by Drago (Rose). T—4:01. A—35,205.

They took their case to the Players Association and it went to arbitration under terms of the Basic Agreement between the owners and the players. Peter Seitz, an arbitrator, heard the case and on December 23, 1975, declared that a player who plays out his contract by not signing for a year is no longer bound to a team.

The decision changed the business of baseball and the future of Pete Rose.

Seitz's ruling resulted in a bitter collective bargaining struggle between the players and the owners. The players claimed the decision applied to everyone and that there was no longer any such thing as a reserve clause. The owners argued that the decision applied to only those two individuals.

When no agreement could be reached the owners refused to allow spring training camps to open in 1976. Eventually, commissioner Bowie Kuhn ordered spring training camps opened and an agreement between the two sides was finally reached whereby a player could become a free agent after six years.

Top: Rose is surrounded by Japanese fans when he arrives for the Reds' first workout in Japan, 1978. *Bottom:* MVP Rose greets Olympic running champion Kip Keino of Kenya in the Olympic Village in Montreal, 1976.

Baseball would never be the same.

The new Basic Agreement had no immediate effect on the Reds. The team continued to dominate, posting a 102–60 mark in 1976 and winning the National League West by 10 games. Rose had another sparkling year, batting .323 and leading the league in hits (215), doubles (42), and runs scored (130).

As good as Rose's season was, however, he was upstaged by Morgan, who hit .320 with 27 homers, 111 RBI, 113 runs scored, and 60 stolen bases to capture his second straight MVP award.

The Reds performance in the post-season competition was devastating. With Rose hitting .429, the "Big Red Machine" swept the Philadelphia Phillies in the National League playoffs. Then, behind an awesome performance by Johnny Bench, who hit .533, they swept the New York Yankees in four straight games to win their second consecutive world championship.

By the following spring, however, cracks were beginning to spread through the Big Red Machine. The age of baseball millionaires had arrived, and the Reds' players wanted their share. Dave Concepcion, Ken Griffey, George Foster, and Johnny Bench all were looking for lucrative, multi-year contracts, and Rose was not happy with the situation.

"Some of these guys want as much money as they're paying me," said Rose. "I worked 14 years to get where I am and they want it after only two or three years. Our guys need to be realistic about this thing."

Rose, though, was having his own contract problems with management, and it was in February of 1977 that he first hinted he might play out his option and leave the Reds.

"If I can get almost double the money from some other club than I'm making with the Reds, I don't see why I shouldn't," he said. "I just don't think a Cincinnati player shouldn't make as much money as some of the other players. It just doesn't make sense that five or six other players are making a lot more money than the top players on our club. We've got the best team in baseball."

THE DYNASTY SWAYS, THEN TOPPLES

The Reds, though, were not the best team in baseball in 1977. They weren't even the best team in the National League West. Although Rose hit .311 and had more than 200 hits (204) for the ninth time to tie Cobb's record, the Reds finished second in the division, 10 games behind the Dodgers.

One of the major reasons for the club's decline was a front office decision to trade the popular Perez before the season began. Perez not only was a solid run producer but was invaluable in the clubhouse where his sense of humor and good nature helped relieve tension.

Rose didn't know it at the time, but the trading

Always a competitor, even when his team is down, Rose competes with a fan for a foul ball.

of Perez was the beginning of the dismantling of The Big Red Machine.

The Reds finished second to the Dodgers again in 1978, but Rose achieved two personal milestones that year. He became a member of the 3,000-hit club on May 5 when he collected two hits off Montreal's Steve Rogers and later that summer set a National League record by hitting in 44 consecutive games.

Rose began his hitting streak on June 14 against Dave Roberts of Chicago. He broke the modern National League record (post 1900) by hitting in his 38th consecutive game on July 25 against Craig Swan of New York and he tied the all-time NL record of 44 straight games set by Willie Keeler in 1897 on July 31 against Phil Niekro of Atlanta. Rose's streak ended on August 1 when he was stopped by Atlanta's Larry McWilliams and Gene Garber.

In his final at-bat of the game, Rose struck out on a 2-2 changeup thrown by Garber and later criticized the Atlanta right-hander for pitching "like it was the seventh game of the World Series." The Braves were leading 16-4 at the time, and Rose felt Garber was trying too hard to rub it in.

"I have an idea that if I was pitching like it was the seventh game of the World Series, he was hitting like it was the ninth inning of the seventh game of the World Series," said Garber. "I wanted his streak to continue but I wanted to get him out, too. That's what I get paid to do."

Rose finished the year with a .302 batting average and a league-leading 51 doubles, but it was to be his final season with the Reds.

That winter, disappointed at the club's contract offer and hard-line attitude, Rose played out his option and signed with the Philadelphia Phillies. His signature on the Philadelphia contract marked the end of an era for one of baseball's greatest teams.

Above: Rose tips his hat to the cheering fans after he ties Tommy Holmes's National League record of hitting in 37 consecutive games, July 24, 1978. *Right:* The streak ends at 44—a dejected Rose walks to the dugout after failing to get a hit in game 45, August 3, 1978.

5

THE FREE AGENT

On the day Pete Rose signed with the Philadelphia Phillies, even the federal government did a double-take.

It wasn't the fact Rose was no longer wearing the uniform of the Cincinnati Reds. It was the four-year, $3.2 million contract he signed with the Phillies that had the U.S. government aghast.

Rose, now the highest paid player in baseball, had thrown President Carter's inflation fighters a curve. The President had instituted an austerity program and asked corporations to keep their salaries within a 7½ percent wage hike limit. How could the administration expect citizens to work toward curbing inflation when one of its most famous citizens was quadrupling his salary?

While the government wasn't too happy about the money being given to Rose, the Phillies felt he was worth every penny. The Phillies had won three straight National League East titles but had been beaten in the playoffs each year. Although Rose was 37 years old, the Phillies were confident he was the player who could put them into a World Series.

They were right about him, only it took one year longer than expected.

As surprising as it might seem, money was not the reason Rose chose the Phillies. In fact, the Pirates, Cardinals, Braves, and Royals all offered Rose more money. Rose chose the Phillies because they offered him not only the opportunity to break Stan Musial's National League record for most career hits but also another chance to play on a championship team.

"What they don't have is an everyday player with playoff experience and World Series experience," said Rose. "I'll try to lead the Philadelphia Phillies straight ahead in every direction."

Rose gave the Phillies their money's worth in his first season with them. In spite of a number of personal problems, including a divorce from his wife, Karolyn, Rose played in every game, hit .331, and collected more than 200 hits (208) for the 10th time in his career to break Ty Cobb's record.

He also adapted to another new position, first base, and became the first player ever elected to the All-Star team at four different positions.

Despite his efforts, the club finished fourth in the National League East. Too many injuries to key personnel was the main season for the club's poor

In 1979, Rose became a free agent—and the highest paid player in baseball.

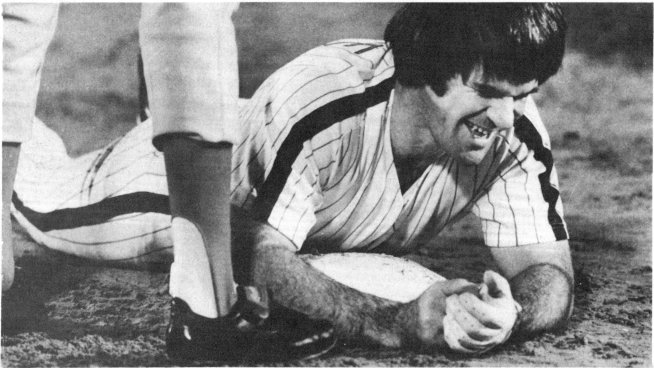

Top: Rose is honored by President Carter in the Oval Office. *Bottom:* Rose, in his new Phillies uniform, films a commercial, 1979. *Right:* Rose acknowledges the cheering crowd after getting his 200th hit of the 1979 season, making it his 10th season with 200 or more hits.

showing. But Rose knew he had signed on with a solid club and he was confident the team would turn around in 1980.

A CROWN FOR THE PHILLIES

He was right. Yet, ironically, the Phillies rise back to the top of the National League East standings came in a year when Rose had his worst season since 1964. Rose hit only .282 yet the Phillies won the division title by one game over Montreal.

Although he failed to hit .300 for only the second time in 16 years, Rose still played in all 162 games, led the league in doubles (42) for the fifth time, scored 95 runs, and collected 185 hits. Those numbers would amount to a great year for most ballplayers, but there was speculation he might be on the way out as an everyday player.

Rose scoffed at such talk and, just as he had done in 1975, proved his critics wrong by leading the Phillies to the National League pennant in a five-game playoff triumph over the Houston Astros.

The playoff series was beautiful. It featured the two mainstays of the now defunct Big Red Machine, Rose and Joe Morgan, on opposite sides of the diamond. They were like a pair of deckhands trying to save their cargo from sinking.

The Phillies had developed a losing mentality in the playoffs and, if Rose hadn't been there to show them how to win, they probably would have lost again. The Astros had never been to the playoffs before and Morgan did all he could to bring them home. In the end, it wasn't quite enough.

The Phillies' Rose puts the tag on Reds' Cesar Geronimo at the start of the 1980 season.

Rose hit .400 in the five-game series, collecting 8 hits in 20 at-bats. He also walked five times and scored three runs. Morgan played in only four of the games, and although he hit only .154, he reached base eight times and had a double and a triple.

Rose hadn't exactly promised the Phillies a world championship when he joined them, but he knew his attitude could help in clutch situations. Rose had always seemed to be in the right place and do the right thing at the right time during his years with Cincinnati. The Phillies knew they could count on him.

He did not let them down. The Phillies defeated the Kansas City Royals in six games to win the first world championship in the history of the franchise and Rose played a pivotal role in the final game.

Although he hit only .261 for the Series and was overshadowed by Mike Schmidt, who won MVP honors, Rose was involved in the most exciting play in the Series and it quite possibly saved the Phillies from an embarrassing loss and a decisive seventh game.

With the Phillies leading 4–1 in the ninth inning of the sixth game, the Royals loaded the bases with one out and Frank White lifted a high pop fly in foul territory that Phillies catcher Bob Boone seemingly had a play on in front of the first base dugout. Boone caught the ball momentarily but it popped out of his glove, and Phillies fans, used to seeing their club crack under pressure in past years, saw it as an omen of certain doom.

But this club was different from previous Phillies teams. It had Rose. He averted the disaster by

Rose and Houston catcher Bruce Bochy slam into each other as Rose scores the go-ahead run in the 10th inning, forcing the Phillies and Astros into a fifth game for the National League pennant.

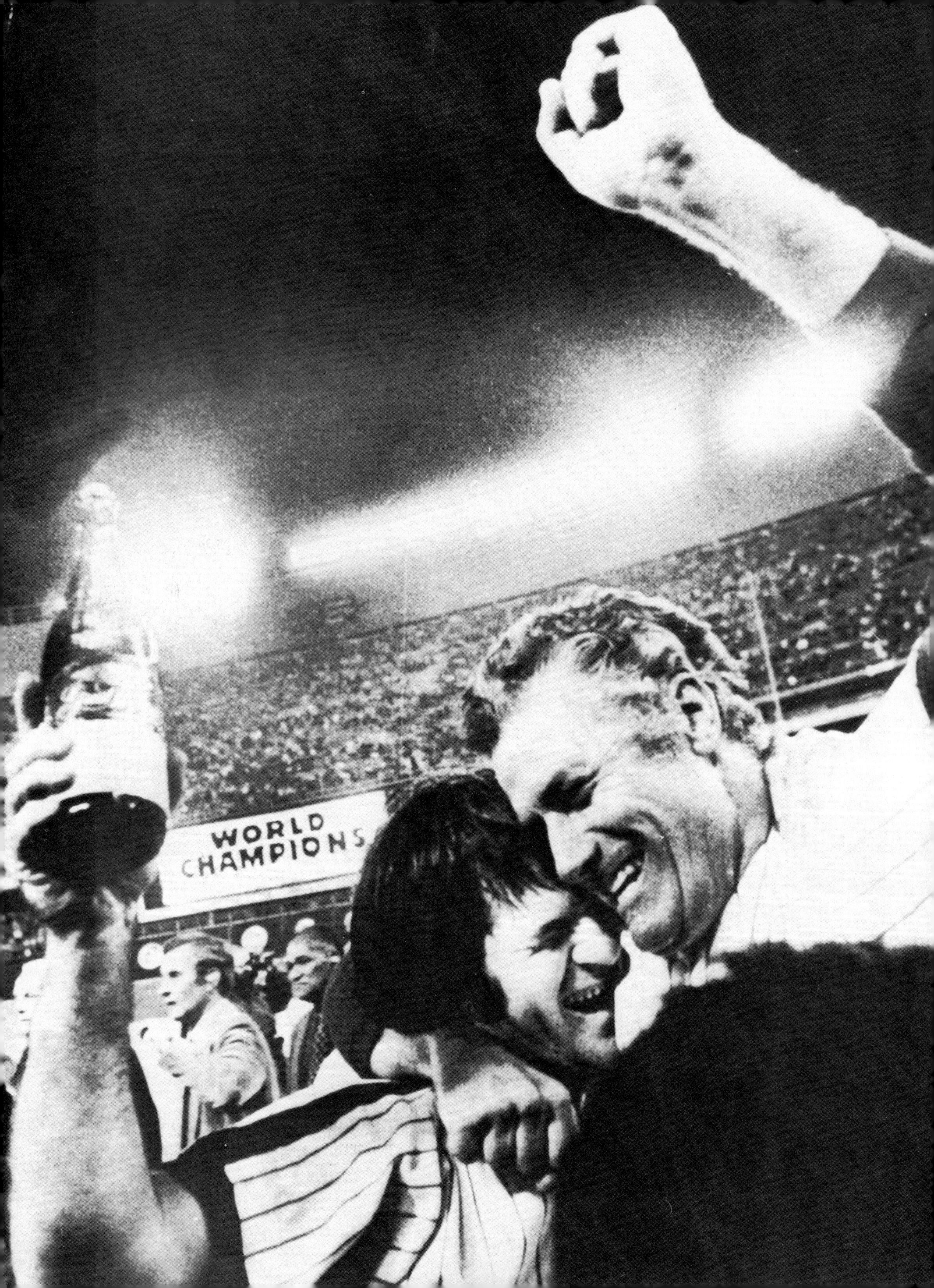
WORLD
CHAMPIONS

Left: A championship for Philadelphia: Rose embraces Phillies manager Dallas Green. *Above:* Rose is all smiles as he looks at the World Championship of Baseball trophy after winning his third World Series, 1980.

Rose stands with the 1,200 bats he signed to commemorate his 10th 200-hit season.

Rose lays down a bunt during spring training.

alertly catching the ball after it popped out of Boone's glove. The next batter, Willie Wilson, struck out and the Phillies—and their star free agent—were world champions.

1981: IT COULD HAPPEN

The year 1981 will live in infamy for many baseball fans. Yet for Pete Rose it was a year of major achievement and one in which he realized that a milestone he once thought unattainable could be conquered.

Mention 1981 and the first thought that comes to the mind of a baseball fan is the labor strike. Many of these fans felt, for the first time, that the modern sport had coldly passed them by. The players called a strike on June 12 that did not end until July 30.

The Phillies played 55 fewer games because of the strike, costing Rose another 200-hit season.

As it turned out, however, he led the league with 140 hits in 107 games and compiled a .325 batting average. Moreover, he surpassed Stan Musial's National League record for most career hits, finishing the year with 3,697. Rose had tied the record on June 10—two days before the strike was called—with a single off Houston's Nolan Ryan and broke it on August 10 with a single off St. Louis's Mark Littell.

During the labor strike, Rose, at 40, worked out just about every day, taking nearly 150 hours of batting practice. He had no idea when baseball would return, but he was determined to be ready.

After Rose broke Musial's record he began thinking seriously about catching Cobb. A few

Rose poses with baseball great Stan Musial at the start of the 1981 season.

The American Cancer Society honors Rose as the Athlete of the Decade.

years before he had not thought Cobb's record was reachable. Now he was eager to try.

"People are worried I might not have a chance to break Cobb's record because I missed 55 games during the strike," said Rose. "Well, if I get that close, I think I will find a way to get it."

Early in his career, Cobb was a phantom with impossible numbers. As the notion dawned that the hit record could be reached, Rose, with typical resolution, began to study his target.

"I can't do it this year. I can't do it next year. But it's definitely something worth thinking about. I probably know more about Ty Cobb than any living player. I've studied his statistics. I know how he played. I know all the Ty Cobb stories.

"To be Number One in the history of your league is tremendous. To be Number One in the history of the game, well, I wasn't much in school so I don't know what the word is."

The strike not only disrupted Rose's hit parade, it turned the season into an abomination. Upon the settlement of the strike, the owners declared that there would be separate champions for each half of the season. The two champions then would meet in a mini-playoff with those winners meeting in the regular playoffs.

As a result of this plan, the Phillies managed to squeeze into the mini-playoffs since they were in first place in the National League East when the strike was called. Montreal won the second half of the season by one-half game over St. Louis.

The real loser, however, was Rose's old team, the Reds. Cincinnati compiled the best overall record in the National League (66–42) but finished second in both halves and did not make the playoffs.

Rose hit .300 against Montreal in the mini-playoffs, but the Expos won the best-of-five series, three games to two, as pitcher Steve Rogers beat the Phillies twice.

The following spring the Phillies extended Rose's contract on a year-to-year basis through 1986 and raised his salary in excess of $1 million a year. As part of the contract, the Phillies had the option to review Rose's performance and status for the following season.

4000 AND THE LEGEND IN SIGHT

Bill Giles, the Phillies' new president, said that Rose would be released if the Phillies decided not to renew his option. However, Giles quickly added that the Phillies had no intention of letting that happen.

Left: Petey Rose, the Phillies' batboy, hangs out in the dugout with his buddy. *Top:* Rose and Stan Musial signal to the crowd after Rose breaks Musial's National League record of 3,630 hits. *Bottom:* An irate Rose argues with the umpire.

In what will forever be carved on the tableau of famous last words, Giles added: "He'll be playing for us when he breaks Ty Cobb's record, whether it's in 1984 or however long it takes."

Rose began his quest of Cobb in earnest in 1982, but he had a disappointing season. Even though he played in all 162 games, he hit .271 and had 172 hits. Despite Rose's subpar season, the Phillies battled St. Louis down to the wire in the NL East but lost out to the Cardinals by three games.

The age question began to be asked again but Rose, naturally, had an answer.

"To be honest with you, I saw the ball good," Rose said of his 1982 campaign. "I was batting second for the first time, and I had a different role. I look at my .271 as a .291."

The Phillies, however, were beginning to have serious doubts. Giles came close to releasing him during late August but changed his mind and Rose hit well in September.

But it was obvious in spring training of 1983 that the Phillies no longer thought of Rose as an everyday player. Although he opened the season as the club's regular first baseman, he was benched for the first time in his career in early June after going 0-for-20 and slumping to .238.

Rose finished the season with a career low .245 average and only 121 hits in 151 games, but the Phillies won the division title again and Rose came alive for the post-season competition. He hit .375 as the Phillies beat the Los Angeles Dodgers in the playoffs and he batted .313 in the World Series, which the Phillies lost to the Baltimore Orioles in five games.

Even though Rose had performed well under the pressure of the post-season competition, the Phillies signaled their intention by benching him for Game 3 of the World Series. He was so upset, he refused interview requests. Within weeks after the end of the World Series, they cut him loose. It hurt Rose deeply.

"When you mess with my pride, when you back me up against the wall with my pride, someone's going to be in trouble," Rose said.

Rose's pride was hurt even more when very few teams expressed interest in him. After three restless months without a team, he joined the Montreal Expos.

Rose managed to convince Expos manager Bill Virdon that he could still do the job on a regular basis, and although he was approaching his 43rd birthday, his name was in the starting lineup on Opening Day. On April 13, 1984, Rose collected another milestone hit—the 4,000th of his career. Ironically, the hit came in a game against the Phillies.

Above: A happy Rose chats with teammates in the dugout after moving into second place for career hits, with 3,772—one more than Hank Aaron. *Right:* Now an Expo, Rose tips his cap to well-wishers in Montreal after career hit Number 4,000.

THE RETURN

The prodigal son returned home on August 16, 1984.

After nearly six years away, Pete Rose came back to his birthplace and put on the uniform in which he had known his greatest glories.

When Rose left the Cincinnati Reds, he never expected to be back. He felt the Reds had betrayed his devotion by not rewarding him with what he felt he was worth.

Rose had not expected to come back, but he had always wanted to. Sentiment aside, it was the quest for the Cobb record that brought him back. And, for the Reds, it was the stuff of which the modern game is made—money.

The groundwork for Rose's return actually began in 1983 when Bob Howsam returned as club president. Although Howsam had no great love for Rose, he knew a good business deal when he saw it.

Pete Rose was the most popular player in Reds' history, the fans loved him, and the box office needed a good boost.

The Reds began negotiations with Montreal to bring Rose back to Cincinnati early in the summer of 1984. Initially, Howsam approached Rose strictly about managing but Rose balked at that offer. Cobb's record had now become an obsession with him and he did not want to give up the chase now that he was so close and had come so far.

"I felt that was the way to go," said Howsam. "You have to want that aspect of the job strong enough that you're willing to do just that. Not play. Just manage. Pete convinced me that he was sincere."

Rose, however, said he would only take the job if he could be a player-manager and Howsam agreed. Besides, Rose going for Ty Cobb's record in the city where he was born was a natural box office bonanza.

Rose watches the ball fall for a RBI single during his first at-bat as the Reds' new player-manager.

Rose's Milestone Hits

No.	Date	Type	Pitcher	Opponent
1	4-13-63	Triple	Bob Friend	Pittsburgh
500	9-16-65	Single	Al Jackson	at New York
1,000	6-26-68	Single	Dick Selma	New York
1,500	8-29-70	Single	Carl Morton	at Montreal
2,000	6-19-73	Single	Ron Bryant	at San Francisco
2,500	8-17-75	Single	Bruce Kison	Pittsburgh
3,000	5- 5-78	Single	Steve Rogers	Montreal
3,500	8-15-80	Single	Tom Hausman	at New York
3,631*	8-10-81	Single	Mark Littell	St. Louis
3,772**	6-22-82	Double	John Stuper	at St. Louis
4,000	4-13-84	Double	Jerry Koosman	Philadelphia

*Sets all-time N.L. record
**Moves into second place ahead of Hank Aaron

The Expos, not exactly ecstatic over the way Rose had performed while with them (.259 in 95 games) and eager to unload his high salary, agreed to send Rose back to Cincinnati in exchange for infielder Tom Lawless. On August 16, Rose replaced Vern Rapp as manager of the Cincinnati Reds.

Rose had come back several times from decline, from off years, and had often disproved predictions that age had caught him. This comeback was different. Rose was reborn. The fountain in downtown Cincinnati really was the Fountain of Youth.

Rose managed the final 41 games of the season and played in 26 of them, batting an incredible .365 with 35 hits in 96 at-bats. He had seven three-hit games and three two-hit games among his 23 starts.

The Reds had a 13–10 record in games that Rose started and he reached base safely via a hit or walk in all 23 of them. He finished the season needing only 95 hits to hit his final goal—4192. He also collected his 726th career double on the last day of the season, setting a National League record and moving into second place on the all-time most doubles list behind Tris Speaker's 793.

What's more, Rose's leadership impressed the young Cincinnati players. One of Rose's oldest friends from the glory days of the Big Red Machine, Tony Perez, observed that virtually all the Reds players relished the opportunity to impress a living legend.

"They wanted to be congratulated by Rose," said Perez. "It's more of a thrill to be congratulated by Pete Rose than Vern Rapp.

"We didn't have everybody giving 100 percent before and I think that was because some guys didn't like the manager. Everybody respects Pete."

Rose's words about his father seem appropriate to explain how the young Cincinnati players were inspired by their new manager.

"It was exposure. I was exposed to him. Fortunately, he played the game right. That's the main reason I've been able to develop all the things that I think are the right way to play the game, the right way to practice, the dedication factor, the 'be on

Above: Rose gets some free advice from longtime friends Dave Concepcion and Tony Perez before taking the field as the Reds player-manager for the first time, August 17, 1984. *Right:* A variety of emotions play across new manager Rose's face as he watches his Cincinnati players and teammates.

time' factor, a lot of little things that lead up to big things. Most of the time, if you do the little things they'll make you win."

Rose started the 1985 season playing often, but in his new role as manager he was able, for the first time in his career, to gracefully relinquish the two decade-long battle to be "the everyday player." As the season progressed and the team started to improve, Rose reduced his playing time and concentrated more on managing.

Still, the name Cobb never left his mind.

During spring training when a sportswriter suggested that some people might think it unfair to compare Cobb's record with Rose's since Rose had played so many more games, the Cincinnati Kid bristled.

"Hey, he played 24 years, didn't he," said Rose. "Evidently, he must have taken too many games off. Consistency is the name of the game. I might be first soon in hits, but I'm also first on the list of making outs. Look at Mantle, fifteen hundred and something strikeouts. That means he was there

every day."

Rose also was certain the general public was pulling for him to break the record. He was reminded that the fans were against Roger Maris when he broke Babe Ruth's single season home run record in 1961, but Rose didn't think the two situations were comparable.

"I think it's different in my case," Rose said. "I think people want to see me break the record 'cause I play like the old-time ballplayer. It seems everybody hated Ty Cobb. I keep reading where nobody came to his funeral."

Not surprisingly, one of Rose's detractors is James H. Cobb, son of the legendary Ty Cobb. In June, James Cobb, the youngest of Ty Cobb's five children, came forth and insisted that major league baseball place an asterisk next to Rose's name when he became baseball's all-time hit leader.

Ford Frick, commissioner of baseball when Maris broke Ruth's record, had insisted an asterisk be placed next to Maris's name that year since he had achieved the mark over a 162-game season instead

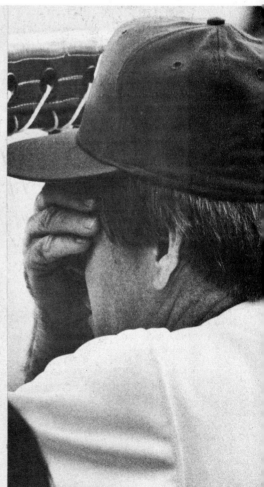

of the 154 games of Ruth's day.

Cobb's son pointed out that Rose also benefitted from a 162-game schedule compared to the 154-game season of his father's time. He also contended that Rose had enjoyed other advantages of the modern game, including better equipment and improved travel accommodations.

Cobb said his analysis of the records shows that Rose had collected 195 of his career hits after the 154th game of the seasons Rose has played. Rose's major league career began after the majors already had adopted the 162-game schedule.

"If Pete Rose had the same schedule my father had, Pete wouldn't even have 4,000 hits yet," said Cobb. "Now I don't want this to sound like sour grapes or anything, but the word 'record' is used too loosely today."

Ty Cobb needed 3,034 games and 11,429 career at-bats to establish baseball's career record for hits. By the time Rose has collected the magical hit, he will have played somewhere in the neighborhood of 3,470 games and had 13,730 at-bats.

Cobb was forced to admit, however, that he admired Rose's style of play.

"He's very much like my father," Cobb said. "He would have admired Pete's determination."

Cobb couldn't say for sure, though, whether his father would have approved of the manner in which his record was being broken.

"Maybe he would say it's all right. Maybe he wouldn't. I do know this: he was proud of his records."

Rose, though, is proud of his too, and he questioned whether Ty Cobb could hit as well in the modern era.

"I doubt that his lifetime .367 batting average would hold up in modern-day baseball," Rose said. "If Ty Cobb came up in 1963 like I did, he'd have a batting average of about .320. (Roberto) Clemente finished at .317. You can't convince me Cobb would have 50 points more than Clemente. Ty Cobb never played at 5:30 [twilight]."

Above: Ty Cobb with his son James H. Cobb, 1943. *Right:* The intensity shows on Rose's face as he embarks on his 23rd season—and his pursuit of 4,192.

Rose loses the ball during practice.

But he snags the ball between his legs in the game.

ON THE WHOLE I'D PREFER TO MEET BABE RUTH

As the inevitable record-breaking game approaches, Cobb's presence may seem closer for the fans. But Rose talks like a man simply gliding the last few steps up the mountain.

Cobb? That's been dealt with and it's all but over. "The first time Cobb made an impression on me was when my name started being mentioned along with his when I began getting 200 hits a season on a regular basis. That's because he had the record of nine seasons of 200 hits and 200 hits was my goal every year. That's the first recollection I have of Cobb.

"But not even three, four, or five years ago did I think about breaking Cobb's hit record. I was just playing every day, trying to play hard.

"I got to know a lot of things about Cobb through my association with Lew Fonseca, who was a hitting instructor, and Waite Hoyt, who was an announcer. They both played against him and knew a lot about him. I was interested in old-time ballplayers, anyway. The more they talked about him, the more I listened.

Then Rose was asked what would he say if he had the chance to meet Cobb. He fired Cobb's ghost a definite shrug. "You know, this sounds strange, but if I had my wish, I would rather meet Babe Ruth than Cobb. I just think Babe Ruth was

Above: The legendary Babe Ruth. *Right:* Ruth hits a big one. *Far right:* The wizened face of Ty Cobb near the end of his career.

the greatest baseball player ever to play. I believe Babe Ruth is a lot responsible for giving guys like me a chance to play.

"That's because just by his presence on the field, he saved baseball many, many times. He saved a lot of franchises. Because of his saving franchises, he gave us all an opportunity to play baseball. No other player could do that.

"I think Babe Ruth was the most dominant force ever to play this game. I would have liked to have met Cobb, too, but if I had a choice of meeting Cobb or Ruth, I think I'd rather meet Ruth."

OLD-TIME PLAYERS, OLD LOVES

Although the hit record is the one mark which will be synonymous with his name, Rose is more proud of three other statistics that can't be found in his list of achievements.

"You know the three stats I'm most proud of that aren't in the press guide? I got the highest average of games played per season, the highest average of hits per season, and the highest average of 600 at-bats per season," Rose said. "Did you know I played in more winning games than Joe DiMaggio played in games? Consistency."

Pete Rose reminds us all of another time when the grass was real, the uniforms were dirty, and the game was played strictly for love, not money. These days he is also reminding us of Cobb, who for all his rage, may also be closer to the sheer joy

Top: Rose's son, 2½, clowns around the infield tarp at Riverfront Stadium. *Bottom:* Karolyn Rose and son Petey cheer dad on during a 1979 game. *Right:* Devoted dad Rose and son Petey relax during an exhibition game.

PETE ROSE, YEAR-BY-YEAR
BY UNITED PRESS INTERNATIONAL

Year	Team	AB	H	2B	3B	HR	R	RBI	SB	AVG.
1963	Cincinnati	623	170	25	9	6	101	41	13	.273
1964	Cincinnati	516	139	13	2	4	64	34	4	.269
1965	Cincinnati	670	209	35	11	11	117	81	8	.312
1966	Cincinnati	654	205	38	5	16	97	70	4	.313
1967	Cincinnati	585	176	32	8	12	86	76	11	.301
1968	Cincinnati	626	210	42	6	10	94	49	3	.335
1969	Cincinnati	627	218	33	11	16	120	82	7	.348
1970	Cincinnati	649	205	37	9	15	120	52	12	.316
1971	Cincinnati	632	192	27	4	13	86	44	13	.304
1972	Cincinnati	645	198	31	11	6	107	57	10	.307
1973	Cincinnati	680	230	36	8	5	115	64	10	.338
1974	Cincinnati	652	185	45	7	3	110	51	2	.284
1975	Cincinnati	662	210	47	4	7	112	74	0	.317
1976	Cincinnati	665	215	42	6	10	130	63	9	.323
1977	Cincinnati	655	204	38	7	9	95	64	16	.311
1978	Cincinnati	655	198	51	3	7	103	52	13	.302
1979	Philadelphia	628	208	40	5	4	90	59	20	.331
1980	Philadelphia	655	185	41	1	1	95	64	12	.282
1981	Philadelphia	431	140	18	5	0	73	33	4	.325
1982	Philadelphia	634	172	25	4	3	80	54	8	.271
1983	Philadelphia	493	121	14	3	0	52	45	7	.245
1984	Montreal-Cincinnati	374	107	15	2	0	43	34	1	.286
Totals		**13411**	**4097**	**726**	**131**	**158**	**2090**	**1243**	**187**	**.305**

in sport than most modern players. Closer even, to Rose.

"I think the main reason I've been able to catch Cobb in hits is my durability. And I say durability and that's funny because Cobb played 24 years. But it's got to be durability. Durability and enthusiasm. Being able to switch-hit helped me, too. When you're a switch-hitter, it helps you hit against relief pitchers. Relief pitching is tough today, and it's been tough the last 15 years. I don't think relief pitching was emphasized when Cobb played like it is today.

"Cobb was known as a very mean individual. Fighting mean. I've had people tell me he was the toughest individual they ever knew. I don't know if he played the game trying to hurt people, but he played the game hard and I try to play the game hard."

"The main similarity we had is we both loved to hit and hate to lose."

Rose is the perennial sandlot kid, the embodiment of a spirit that makes little children of us all and lightens our load. He symbolizes not simply the work ethic but the joy in work. And he shows us how far perseverance and desire can take us.

In an era of high-priced prima donnas, artificial-surface fields, and domed stadiums, we need this exuberant, durable Rose.

Right: With the same determination and drive he displays here, Rose pursues Ty Cobb's record. He will let no obstacle stand in his way.

APPENDIX
THE PETE ROSE STATISTICS

Championship Series

Year Team	G	AB	R	H	2B	3B	HR	RBI	BB	SO	SB	AVG.
1970 Cincinnati vs. Pittsburgh	3	13	1	3	0	0	0	1	0	0	0	.231
1972 Cincinnati vs. Pittsburgh	5	20	1	9	4	0	0	2	1	2	0	.450
1973 Cincinnati vs. New York	5	21	3	8	1	0	2	2	2	2	0	.381
1975 Cincinnati vs. Pittsburgh	3	14	3	5	0	0	1	2	0	2	0	.357
1976 Cincinnati vs. Philadelphia	3	14	3	6	2	1	0	2	1	0	0	.429
1980 Philadelphia vs. Houston	5	20	3	8	0	0	0	2	5	3	0	.400
1983 Philadelphia vs. Los Angeles	4	16	3	6	0	0	0	0	1	1	1	.375
Totals	**28**	**118**	**17**	**45**	**7**	**1**	**3**	**11**	**10**	**10**	**1**	**.381**

World Series

Year Team	G	AB	R	H	2B	3B	HR	RBI	BB	SO	SB	AVG.
1970 Cincinnati vs. Baltimore	5	20	2	5	1	0	1	2	2	0	0	.250
1972 Cincinnati vs. Oakland	7	28	3	6	0	0	1	2	4	4	1	.214
1975 Cincinnati vs. Boston	7	27	3	10	1	1	0	2	5	1	0	.370
1976 Cincinnati vs. New York	4	16	1	3	1	0	0	1	2	2	0	.188
1980 Philadelphia vs. Kansas City	6	23	2	6	1	0	0	1	2	2	0	.261
1983 Philadelphia vs. Baltimore	5	16	1	5	1	0	0	1	1	3	0	.313
Totals	**34**	**130**	**12**	**35**	**5**	**1**	**2**	**9**	**16**	**12**	**1**	**.269**

All-Star Game

Year Team, Site	G	AB	R	H	2B	3B	HR	RBI	BB	SO	SB	AVG.
1965 NL. Minneapolis	1	2	0	0	0	0	0	0	1	2	0	.000
1967 NL. California	1	1	0	0	0	0	0	0	0	0	0	.000
1968 NL. Houston	Injured, did not play											
1969 NL. Washington	1	1	0	0	0	0	0	0	0	0	0	.000
1970 NL. Cincinnati	1	3	1	1	0	0	0	0	1	2	0	.333
1971 NL. Detroit	1	0	0	0	0	0	0	0	0	0	0	.000
1973 NL. Kansas City	1	3	1	0	0	0	0	0	1	0	0	.000
1974 NL. Pittsburgh	1	2	0	0	0	0	0	0	0	1	0	.000
1975 NL. Milwaukee	1	4	0	2	0	0	0	1	0	0	0	.500
1976 NL. Philadelphia	1	3	1	2	0	1	0	0	0	0	0	.667
1977 NL. New York (A)	1	2	0	0	0	0	0	0	0	0	0	.000
1978 NL. San Diego	1	4	0	1	1	0	0	0	0	0	0	.250
1979 NL. Seattle	1	2	0	0	0	0	0	0	0	0	0	.000
1980 NL. Los Angeles	1	1	0	0	0	0	0	0	0	0	0	.000
1981 NL. Cleveland	1	3	0	1	0	0	0	0	0	0	0	.333
1982 NL. Montreal	1	1	0	0	0	0	0	1	0	0	0	.000
Totals	**15**	**32**	**3**	**7**	**1**	**1**	**0**	**2**	**3**	**5**	**0**	**.219**

Career vs. the National League

	AB	H	HR	RBI	AVG.		AB	H	HR	RBI	AVG.
Atlanta	1418	460	25	152	.324	Chicago	1250	382	18	124	.306
Cincinnati	257	74	1	22	.288	Montreal	805	243	7	61	.302
Houston	1388	436	9	135	.314	New York	1243	377	11	101	.303
Los Angeles	1331	381	20	112	.286	Philadelphia	965	326	13	92	.338
San Diego	940	282	8	84	.300	Pittsburgh	1227	359	15	112	.293
San Francisco	1322	398	17	135	.301	St. Louis	1265	379	14	113	.300
N.L. West	**6656**	**2031**	**80**	**640**	**.305**	**N.L. East**	**6755**	**2066**	**78**	**603**	**.306**

Rose's Game Highs

Hits: 5 (9 times): most recent: 4/28/82 at
Los Angeles (for Philadelphia)

HR: 3: 4/29/78 at New York
2 (4 times): most recent: 8/9/70 at
Los Angeles

RBI: 6: 7/18/64 vs. Philadelphia

SB: 3 (2 times): most recent: 5/11/80 at Cincinnati
(for Philadelphia)

Hitting Streak: 44 games: 6/14-7/31/78

Grand Slam: 7/18/64 vs. Philadelphia off Green

4,192—Peter Edward Rose has come a long way.

PETE ROSE'S MILESTONES
BY UNITED PRESS INTERNATIONAL

1960—At age 19, signed with Cincinnati Reds after his uncle, a pro scout, convinced club officials to give him a tryout.

1963—Broke into the majors as a second baseman.

1963—Recorded his first big league hit with a triple off Pittsburgh's Bob Friend at Crosley Field.

1963—Named National League Rookie of the Year after hitting .273.

1965—Hit .300 for the first time, finishing at .312.

1968—Singled off Dick Selma of the Mets for his 1,000th career hit.

1968—Won the National League batting title with a .335 average, going 5-for-5 off San Francisco's Gaylord Perry in the next-to-last game of the season.

1969—Won his second straight batting title with a career-high .348 average.

1970—Was the last player to get a hit at Crosley Field (triple off San Francisco's Juan Marichal) and became the first Cincinnati player to get a hit in the new Riverfront Stadium, singling off Pat Jarvis of Atlanta in a 4-for-5 day.

1972—Led the league in games, at-bats, and hits.

1973—Won his third batting title with a .338 average on a career high 230 hits and was named the league's Most Valuable Player for the first time.

1973—Reached the 2,000-hit mark with a single off San Francisco's Ron Bryant at Candlestick Park.

1975—Registered hit 2,500 against Bruce Kison of Pittsburgh at Riverfront.

1975—Named the World Series' Most Valuable Player after hitting .370 (10-for-27) as the Reds won their first world championship in 35 years.

1977—Passed Frankie Frisch as the all-time switch hitter with his 2,881st hit at St. Louis.

1977—Hit .300 for the 12th time in 13 years and equaled Ty Cobb's major league record by getting 200 or more hits in a season for the ninth time.

1978—On opening day, broke Frank McCormick's club record by playing in 653rd consecutive game.

1978—Hit three home runs in one game for the first time in his career in a 5-for-6 performance against the New York Mets.

1978—Got 3,000th career hit off Montreal's Steve Rogers.

1978—Hit in 44 straight games to set modern National League record.

1980—Collected 3,500th career hit with single off Tom Hausman of New York.

1981—Set all-time National League record for most hits (3,631) with single off Mark Littell of St. Louis.

1982—Moves into second place on all-time hit list ahead of Hank Aaron with double off John Stuper of St. Louis.

PETE ROSE WITH THE BAT AND THE GLOVE

When Pete Rose joined the majors, he did not strike anyone as a fine fielder. But, as in all other phases of his game, he worked on his weaknesses until they disappeared. The chart below shows that his fielding average started at an acceptable .971 and climbed steadily until 1974 when he had a .997 to lead the league in fielding as for right fielders. The following year he shifted to third and his fielding average dropped, but a .963 is good, considering the action that transpires there. One little remarked fact about Rose is that though he has been heralded most for hitting, he has more often led the league with his glove.

PETE ROSE'S BATTING AND FIELDING AVERAGES

		BA	FA
1963	Cincinnati, 2b	.273	.971
1964	Cincinnati, 2b	.269	.979
1965	Cincinnati, 2b	.312	.975
1966	Cincinnati, 2b	.313	.981
1967	Cincinnati, LF	.301	.982
1968	Cincinnati, RF	.335*	.990
1969	Cincinnati, RF	.348*	.988
1970	Cincinnati, RF	.316*	.997
1971	Cincinnati, RF	.304	.994
1972	Cincinnati, LF	.307	.994
1973	Cincinnati, LF	.338*	.992
1974	Cincinnati, LF	.284*	.997
1975	Cincinnati, 3B	.316	.963
1976	Cincinnati, 3B	.323*	.969
1977	Cincinnati, 3B	.311	.958
1978	Cincinnati, 3B	.302	.961
1979	Philadelphia, 1B	.331	.995
1980	Philadelphia, 1B	.282*	.997
1981	Philadelphia, 1B	.325	.996
1982	Philadelphia, 1B	.271	.995
1983	Philadelphia, 1B	.245	.990
1984	Montreal, 1B-OF	.286	.985

*led league